Microsoft Office 365: Exchange Online Implementation and Migration

Implement and migrate to Exchange Online in Office 365

David Greve

Loryan Strant

BIRMINGHAM - MUMBAI

Microsoft Office 365: Exchange Online Implementation and Migration

First published: May 2012

Production Reference: 1180512

Published by Packt Publishing Ltd.
Livery Place
35 Livery Street
Birmingham B3 2PB, UK.

ISBN 978-1-84968-586-3

www.packtpub.com

Cover Image by Will Kewley (william.kewley@kbbs.ie)

Credits

Authors
David Greve

Loryan Strant

Reviewers
Chris Prewitt

Shalini Pasupneti

S. Rene Strawser

Acquisition Editor
Kerry George

Lead Technical Editor
Pramila Balan

Technical Editor
Vrinda Amberkar

Project Coordinators
Kushal Bhardwaj

Theresa Chettiar

Proofreader
Linda Morris

Indexer
Monica Ajmera Mehta

Graphics
Valentina D'Silva

Manu Joseph

Production Coordinators
Alwin Roy

Melywn Dsa

Cover Work
Alwin Roy

Foreword

In the middle of 2006, I was preparing for an important executive review for Jeff Raikes to seek approval to kick off the project to build "CCS"—a communication and collaboration service from Microsoft. As was Jeff's approach to big decision meetings, he would ask for the PowerPoint slides in advance so he could review the content. He would often start the meeting with questions about the plan instead of following the carefully crafted storyline we would build with our slides. This approval meeting was no different, but how he started the meeting was certainly unique. As the group of us working on the project and the other execs from the division settled into their seats for the two-hour review, Jeff open the meeting with a question: "Is there anyone in the room who doesn't think we should do this?" For the next few moments, the room was silent. With a smile on his face, Jeff jumped back in again by saying "Let's do it." What was scheduled to be a two-hour meeting, lasted for 45 minutes and CCS was born.

CCS launched as the Business Productivity Online Suite (BPOS) in 2008, later became Office 365 in 2011 and now is one of the fastest growing businesses in Microsoft's history. The reasons why the business is growing so quickly now, are the same reasons why Jeff was so quick to approve the project—Office 365 creates value for customers, it created value for Microsoft and it creates value for partners. It is rare that a new business can create so much value across the ecosystem, but when it happens, things take off—Office 365 is a great example of that dynamic.

The virtuous fly wheel starts with the customer. If there isn't value for the customer, then the business can't get off the ground. The value to customers is relatively straight forward: with Office 365 they will save money, simplify their overall IT environment, see higher reliability and tighter security, while providing their end users with the best productivity experience that is always up-to-date.

For Microsoft, Office 365 allows us to expand into new markets, serve new customers and reduce churn by delivering a better overall experience using our latest technology. Office 365 makes technologies such as SharePoint, previously only available to the largest enterprises, now available to small and midsized businesses. By staying up-to-date with the latest bits, Office 365 keeps customers on our latest products and it improves overall loyalty to Microsoft through a better customer experience. These factors have motivated Microsoft to continue to make deeper and deeper investments in Office 365 moving forward.

Finally, Office 365 has created a great opportunity for partners to help customers fully capture the value of Office 365 as they use the service. Office 365 helps partners scale to reach new customers and deliver higher level value. Less time and effort is spent setting up servers, and more time can be spent customizing the environment to meet the needs of the customer. Partners can help customers in two key ways:

- Migrating from their current environment into Office 365 and once they have Office 365 up and running
- Customizing the environment to meet the needs of the customer's business

While the value proposition of Office 365 may be clear, getting there isn't always straightforward. This book represents an excellent resource for people with basic IT skills who are looking to move to Office 365, but aren't sure of how to get started. The authors, David Greve and Loryan Strant, are both Office 365 MVPs, and experts in helping customers take full advantage of moving to, and using Office 365.

Enjoy the book, Office 365, and welcome to the cloud.

Eron Kelly
General Manager
Microsoft Corporation

About the Authors

David Greve is a Microsoft Office 365 MVP and Microsoft Certified Professional with more than 15 years of IT consulting experience, specifically around the design and implementation of Microsoft Solutions ranging from small to enterprise environments. One of David's current ventures is designing and developing Microsoft Cloud Computing (BPOS and Office 365) solutions with an emphasis on Exchange Online, SharePoint Online and Lync Online, as well as strategic migration planning in complex business environments. Before directing his focus and concentration to Microsoft Cloud Computing solutions, David worked with Active Directory infrastructure design, on-premise Exchange deployments and migrations, and on-premise SharePoint architecture.

David has been working with PointBridge, now Perficient, since 2005 and is currently leading their Office 365 business. PointBridge is an IT consulting firm that specializes in building high-impact business solutions with Microsoft technology. Headquartered in Chicago, Illinois with offices in Milwaukee, Wisconsin and Boston, Massachusetts, PointBridge is one of the fastest growing Microsoft partners in the central United States and is a National Systems Integrator (NSI).

I would like to thank my colleagues at PointBridge for their support and guidance on various use cases and scenarios I've presented in this book. I would also like to thank the PointBridge leadership team for the outstanding support and flexibility to work on exciting new opportunities within the business and in my personal life. Most importantly, I would like to thank my family for their support as I pursue ways to expand my passion for technology and contributions to the community.

Loryan Strant is veteran of web and network technologies since fifteen years. He has spent the last decade and a half building digital relationships for businesses and organizations. Loryan blogs at `thecloudmouth.com` and writes articles for BoxFreeIT (`boxfreeit.com.au`) and a variety of other sites.

Loryan is also the founder of a leading Australian cloud engineering company Paradyne—helping to deliver innovative solutions through the cloud, enabling businesses to reduce fixed IT costs. He is passionate about enabling people and organizations using technology the right way, enabling them to become more productive.

Some of the company's notable successes include being an Microsoft Australian Partner Award finalist for Online Services, delivering the first Windows Intune customer in Australia, launching the first marketplace in the world for BPOS third-party solutions, delivering the first Office 365 customer in Australia and becoming the first Office 365 MVP in Australia.

In April 2011, Loryan became the first Microsoft Office 365 MVP in Australia. His passion for technology has also enabled him to deliver the first customers in Australia for Office 365 (commercial and educational) and Windows Intune.

Previously, Loryan held Senior Consultant and Project Manager roles at Brennan IT and SKILLED Group. He worked as a Convergence Design Consultant at BTAS and as a Senior Solutions Consultant for Total Network Support. He has achieved several Microsoft certifications, including Office Communications Server 2007 and Microsoft Certified Systems Engineer (MCSE).

I would like to thank my amazing wife for giving me the time to write this book and for the patience while I wrote it.

About the Reviewers

Chris Prewitt is a Senior Technical Consultant on the Unified Communications team at Perficient. Over the past fifteen years, Chris worked with medium business and enterprise clients on a wide variety of messaging co-existence and migration projects.

Shalini Pasupneti is a Senior Consultant focusing on Office 365 and Exchange at Perficient. She has more than 8 years of experience in IT and Healthcare. She holds MCITP for Exchange 2010, MCTS for Lync and CCNA.

Rene Strawser has been engaged in the Information Technology field for over 18 years, working as a senior consultant for the past 11 years. Rene's diverse experience includes leading all stages of directory and messaging solutions with system development efforts, including requirements definition, architecture design, planning, and implementations with organizations of varying sizes. Her recent engagements have included FIM 2010 implementations, Exchange solutions, co-existence, and deployments including migrations to BPOS/Office 365. In addition to work experience, she holds MCSE, MCTS, and MCITP for Exchange, and is also ITIL 3 Certified.

Rene resides with her two children in the Columbus area. In her free time, she enjoys laughing with her children, cycling, and shoes!

www.PacktPub.com

Support files, eBooks, discount offers and more

You might want to visit www.PacktPub.com for support files and downloads related to your book.

Did you know that Packt offers eBook versions of every book published, with PDF and ePub files available? You can upgrade to the eBook version at www.PacktPub.com and as a print book customer, you are entitled to a discount on the eBook copy. Get in touch with us at service@packtpub.com for more details.

At www.PacktPub.com, you can also read a collection of free technical articles, sign up for a range of free newsletters and receive exclusive discounts and offers on Packt books and eBooks.

http://PacktLib.PacktPub.com

Do you need instant solutions to your IT questions? PacktLib is Packt's online digital book library. Here, you can access, read and search across Packt's entire library of books.

Why Subscribe?

- Fully searchable across every book published by Packt
- Copy and paste, print and bookmark content
- On demand and accessible via web browser

Free Access for Packt account holders

If you have an account with Packt at www.PacktPub.com, you can use this to access PacktLib today and view nine entirely free books. Simply use your login credentials for immediate access.

Instant Updates on New Packt Books

Get notified! Find out when new books are published by following @PacktEnterprise on Twitter, or the *Packt Enterprise* Facebook page.

Table of Contents

Preface

The introduction of Office 365 has heralded a new era of productivity for organizations of all types and sizes, wherever they are in the world.

Office 365 provides small businesses with the same level of technology that was previously only affordable to enterprises. For many organizations this can equate to an increase in competitive advantage.

For enterprises Office 365 allows them to move operationally important systems such as e-mail out to the cloud with Exchange Online—to be maintained and optimized by Microsoft. This allows enterprises to focus on their line of business-enhancing technologies that will empower the organization to achieve greater levels of productivity and efficiency.

Exchange Online is by far the most popular component of Office 365 as it allows organizations of any size to offload their mailbox functionality to Microsoft and focus on their business—instead of having to worry about keeping servers operational and mail flowing.

While Office 365 also includes SharePoint Online, Lync Online, Office Web Apps, and Office Professional Plus, this book will focus specifically on Exchange Online.

What this book covers

In this book we will cover common scenarios for implementing Exchange Online ranging from simple one-way migrations to hybrid environments for co-existence with existing on-premise mail systems.

Chapter 1, Getting Started, covers the differences in Office 365 plans and the basics around obtaining an Office 365 subscription.

Chapter 2, Getting Familiar with the Office 365 Admin Portal, walks you through the administrative interfaces of Office 365 and how to add your first domain name.

Chapter 3, Integration Options for Small Businesses and Professionals, explains what options are available for customers of the "P1" plan to integrate with their on-premise systems.

Chapter 4, Integration Options for Enterprises, explains what options are available for customers of the Enterprise or Exchange only plans and integration with their on-premise systems.

Chapter 5, Preparing for a Simple Migration, helps subscribers of the small business plan to prepare their environment and existing mail systems to ensure that their migration to Exchange Online happens smoothly.

Chapter 6, Performing a Simple Migration, builds on Chapter 5 by explaining the process involved in performing a one-way migration to Exchange Online from a variety of mail systems.

Chapter 7, Preparing for a Hybrid Deployment and Migration, focuses on preparation to your Office 365 subscription and the integration components necessary for a Hybrid deployment.

Chapter 8, Deploying a Hybrid Infrastructure: ADFS, covers technical tasks required to install and configure ADFS for Office 365.

Chapter 9, Deploying a Hybrid Infrastructure: Directory Synchronization, covers technical tasks required to install and configure Directory Synchronization for Office 365.

Chapter 10, Deploying a Hybrid Infrastructure: Exchange Hybrid, covers technical tasks required to install and configure Exchange Hybrid for Office 365.

Chapter 11, Performing a Hybrid Migration, teaches you the necessary steps to perform a migration to Office 365 from both the user interface and through PowerShell.

Chapter 12, Post Migration Considerations, teaches you how to address resources and make a mail routing change by following the implementation and migration to Office 365.

References, where you will find references to further reading or the supporting documentations.

What you need for this book

While the scenarios for small businesses and enterprise migrations may have different requirements they do share some common needs.

As the person performing the migration you will need to ensure that you have administrative access to your existing mail system, a high quality Internet connection, access to make domain name record modifications and patience!

Who this book is for

While Office 365 can make administration of enterprise-grade mail platforms simpler, readers of this book will still require an understanding of how e-mail systems work and familiarity with DNS and various mail platforms.

It is expected that readers will have at least basic IT skills in order to perform a migration to the small business plans. Readers who will be using the enterprise plans and looking at hybrid environments with Exchange Online will need a far greater level of familiarity with Active Directory and Exchange Server.

Ultimately this book can be categorized as being useful for small business owners with some level of technical understanding, through to corporate messaging administrators and IT consultants.

Conventions

In this book, you will find a number of styles of text that distinguish between different kinds of information. Here are some examples of these styles, and an explanation of their meaning.

Code words in text are shown as follows: "Does your monthly Internet download allowance cater for the mailboxes being downloaded back into the Outlook .OST file for each user?"

A block of code is set as follows:

```
$mbxlist = Import-CSV c:\csv\migrationbulk.csv
foreach ($line in $mbxlist) {
New-MoveRequest -Identity $line.alias -Remote -RemoteHostName mail.
pointbridgelab.com -TargetDeliveryDomain pointbridgelab.mail.
onmicrosoft.com -RemoteCredential $RemoteCredential
}
```

When we wish to draw your attention to a particular part of a code block, the relevant lines or items are set in bold:

```
$mbxlist = Import-CSV c:\csv\migrationbulk.csv
foreach ($line in $mbxlist) {
New-MoveRequest -Identity $line.alias -Remote -RemoteHostName mail.
pointbridgelab.com -TargetDeliveryDomain pointbridgelab.mail.
onmicrosoft.com -RemoteCredential $RemoteCredential
}
```

Any command-line input or output is written as follows:

```
$cred = Get-Credential
```

New terms and **important words** are shown in bold. Words that you see on the screen, in menus or dialog boxes for example, appear in the text like this: "To add your domain to Office 365, click on the **Domains** menu option on the left".

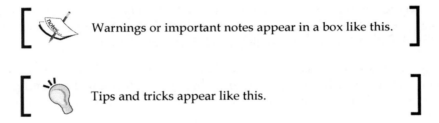

> Warnings or important notes appear in a box like this.

> Tips and tricks appear like this.

Reader feedback

Feedback from our readers is always welcome. Let us know what you think about this book—what you liked or may have disliked. Reader feedback is important for us to develop titles that you really get the most out of.

To send us general feedback, simply send an e-mail to feedback@packtpub.com, and mention the book title through the subject of your message.

If there is a topic that you have expertise in and you are interested in either writing or contributing to a book, see our author guide on www.packtpub.com/authors.

Customer support

Now that you are the proud owner of a Packt book, we have a number of things to help you to get the most from your purchase.

Errata

Although we have taken every care to ensure the accuracy of our content, mistakes do happen. If you find a mistake in one of our books—maybe a mistake in the text or the code—we would be grateful if you would report this to us. By doing so, you can save other readers from frustration and help us improve subsequent versions of this book. If you find any errata, please report them by visiting http://www.packtpub.com/support, selecting your book, clicking on the **errata submission form** link, and entering the details of your errata. Once your errata are verified, your submission will be accepted and the errata will be uploaded to our website, or added to any list of existing errata, under the Errata section of that title.

Piracy

Piracy of copyright material on the Internet is an ongoing problem across all media. At Packt, we take the protection of our copyright and licenses very seriously. If you come across any illegal copies of our works, in any form, on the Internet, please provide us with the location address or website name immediately so that we can pursue a remedy.

Please contact us at copyright@packtpub.com with a link to the suspected pirated material.

We appreciate your help in protecting our authors, and our ability to bring you valuable content.

Questions

You can contact us at questions@packtpub.com if you are having a problem with any aspect of the book, and we will do our best to address it.

1
Getting Started

Welcome to the world of Office 365 — a new way of increasing productivity by harnessing the power of the cloud.

By reading this chapter you will learn what plans are available for your business, how to decide which option to take, and how to get your Office 365 subscription underway.

Throughout this chapter, we hope to provide you with guidance on how to determine your requirements. We will provide you with information on the choices and the decisions you will need to make. We will also provide you with examples of real world customers on Office 365.

Let's begin by looking at the different options available under Office 365.

- Office 365 plans
- Office 365 for Small Businesses and Professionals – considerations and limitations
- Office 365 for Enterprises
- When to use a plan and when to pick à la carte
- Options to start your subscription
- The sign-up process

Office 365 plans

At the heart of Office 365 are two essential subscription paths a customer can go through:

- Office 365 for Small Businesses and Professionals
- Office 365 for Enterprises

(There is also Office 365 for education which is similar in the feature listing and plans to the enterprise offering, however it is licensed in a way not covered in this book.)

The main difference between the two subscription types is that under the small business and professionals plan, the subscription provides high value but no licensing flexibility. There are also several other limitations which are addressed further in this chapter.

There are a number of different ways to purchase these:

- Directly on the Office 365 administration portal
- From a syndication partner (for example, a telecommunications provider that resells Office 365)
- From a Microsoft licensing reseller (for example, an IT company that supplies Microsoft Open Business or Open Value licenses)
- From a Microsoft Large Account Reseller for those with School/Campus/Select/Enterprise agreements

Navigating the Microsoft licensing maze can be challenging; most people can get quite confused by all the various plans and licensing models.

The best approach is to write down what features and functionality you want for your organization, including your people plans for the next three years. Having this information, you can then look at the Office 365 subscription plans and make the right decisions. If you're still lost, you may need to work with a Microsoft partner who specializes in Office 365 to help you make the right licensing choice.

Office 365 for Small Businesses and Professionals—considerations and limitations

The Office 365 plan for Small Businesses and Professionals provides amazing value and functionality for small and growing organizations. It includes Exchange Online Plan 1, SharePoint Online Plan 1, Lync Online Plan 2, and Office Web Apps. To learn more about the various individual plans, follow this link: `http://www.microsoft.com/en-us/office365/online-services.aspx#fbid=zJh_25lOGc5`.

For many businesses it will provide far more functionality than they may ever utilize, however there are some key limitations that must be considered prior to purchase.

Phone / ticketed support by Microsoft not included

Support is only available via the Office 365 community site. Some syndication partners however may offer level 1 support as part of the subscription (for example, Telstra in Australia).

User count limited and no way to upgrade to an E Plan

There is a hard limit of 50 users in the small business plan and there is no way around it. If you ever need to go above 50 — the entire organization would have to be completely migrated out of Office 365 and back in to a new tenant.

SharePoint limitations

While the SharePoint functionality of the small business plan is relatively on par with the enterprise capabilities there are a few key limitations that may require you to move up plans.

Only two site collections are possible — one for private or *intranet* use and one for the public facing website. This is generally not a concern for most organizations under 50 in size, however it can potentially be an issue for organizations that may have separation of business units and security groups.

Additional storage cannot be purchased. The default storage allocation for SharePoint Online is 10 GB as a base platform plus 500 MB contributed for every user. So if you have 50 users the maximum amount of storage you could possibly have in your site collection is 35 GB (10 GB + (50 x 0.5 GB).

Another limitation is that SSL certificates are not provided or supported, meaning that any traffic between your device and your SharePoint Online site is unencrypted.

Active Directory Synchronization is not supported

If you run an Active Directory environment in your office — you cannot replicate the user accounts to Office 365, and that user and password management will be done separately. Replicating your user's accounts to Office 365 enables you to simplify the overall management of your environment and provisioning of users. Often at times, this is less of an issue for small businesses.

Largely this also means that Active Directory Federation Services (leveraging on-premise Active Directory credentials) is not supported; however this is usually out of the realm of small businesses.

However, if your organization runs Microsoft Small Business Server 2011 Essentials—there is an add-on pack that integrates with Office 365 and synchronizes users and passwords.

No access to Forefront Online Protection for the Exchange (FOPE) console

For small businesses, no access to the **Forefront Online Protection for Exchange (FOPE)** console may not be a great concern, however the FOPE console is the rich management and reporting functionality that allows organizations to understand and manage their e-mail security.

Limited license choice

For customers using the Office 365 for Small Businesses plan—there is no ability to mix and match individual licenses.

Doesn't include e-mail archiving

Unlike the enterprise plans, Office 365 for small businesses does not allow for the addition of a mailbox archive on top of the existing 25 GB mailbox. What is possible however is to segment the existing mailbox into an archive area (for example, 5 GB of your 25 GB) which is only available when online with Outlook or via Outlook Web App.

Doesn't support the Blackberry Enterprise Server

If customers using Office 365 for small businesses use BlackBerry smartphones then the only option available is to use the **BlackBerry Individual Service (BIS)** for synchronization of e-mails wirelessly. This does not support synchronization of calendar and contact items as the **BlackBerry Enterprise Service (BES)** does under the Office 365 for Enterprises plan.

Office 365 for Enterprises

While the plan for small businesses is a fixed license choice, the enterprise license—while also offering feature bundles, allows for much greater licensing flexibility.

The key bundles available range from plans E1—E4, as well as K1 and K2 for lighter users, which are broken down as follows:

Bundle	Features
E1	Exchange Online Plan 1
	SharePoint Online Plan 1
	Lync Online Plan 2
	BlackBerry Enterprise Server
E2	Same as E1 plus
	Office Web Apps
E3	Same as E2 plus
	Office Professional Plus 2010
E4	Same as E3 plus
	Lync Online Voice
K1	Exchange Online Kiosk
	SharePoint Online Plan 1
	Office Web Apps (read only)
K2	Same as K1 but Office Web Apps is fully functional

Individual components can also be purchased:

- Exchange Online Plan 1
- Exchange Online Plan 2
- Exchange Online Archiving
- Exchange Online Kiosk
- SharePoint Online Plan 1
- SharePoint Online Plan 2
- SharePoint Online Additional Storage
- SharePoint Online Partner Access License
- Lync Online Plan 1
- Lync Online Plan 2

- Office Web Apps with SharePoint Online Plan 1
- Office Web Apps with SharePoint Online Plan 1
- Office Professional Plus 2010

When to use a plan and when to pick à la carte

Now that you know a bit more about the small business and enterprise subscription levels, let's delve deeper into helping you make a choice between them.

The enterprise plans contain a similar feature set to the small business plan, but are able to go above and beyond the limitations of the small business plan.

Some key benefits are:

- None of the limitations to the small business plan apply
- No limit on the amount of users
- Ability to mix and match license types

Let's look at some scenarios where you might choose one subscription type over the other:

Scenario	Plan choice
Professional services firm of 6 people: Planning to grow to 30 people within 3 years	small business
Start-up recruitment firm of 10 people: planning to grow to 70 within 2 years	Enterprise: E2
Established audio engineering company of 27 users: Have been operating for 9 years No growth plans	small business
Architectural firm of 12 people: Have been operating for 6 years No growth plans Need storage space for drawings	Enterprise: E1 SharePoint Additional Storage

Scenario	Plan Choice
Call center company with 40 staff:	Enterprise:
10 in the office all day, 5 remote workers	E1 (15)
25 shift-based call center staff who don't have their own PCs and simply need access to e-mail and the company intranet	K1 (25)
Franchise coffee house with 40 staff:	Enterprise:
30 staff at head office	E1 (10)
10 franchise managers	E3 (30)
Want to perform Business Intelligence with SharePoint Server 2010 Enterprise on-premise, let franchise managers access the reports	
Medical services with 120 staff:	Enterprise:
Exchange 2010 on-premise	Lync Online Plan 2 (15)
Using other intranet system	
15 staff require video conferencing	
Hospitality services company with 700 staff:	Enterprise:
Exchange 2003 on-premise	Exchange Online Plan 1 (700)
300 staff at head office	Lync Online Plan 1 (600)
400 staff spread across 8 offices	Lync Online Plan 2 (100)
Legacy phone system, want IM and presence, video conferencing for management	
SharePoint on-premise, heavily integrated with CRM and other systems	
Financial services company of 5,000 staff nationwide	Enterprise:
	E1 (4,500)
Lotus Notes	K2 (500)
25 percent of workforce is permanently mobile	
10 percent of workforce primarily limited to Line of Business Application	
Has Enterprise Agreement which includes Office	
Automotive manufacturer of 30,000 staff globally	Enterprise:
GroupWise	Exchange Online Plan 1 (17,000)
IBM WebSphere for intranet	Exchange Online Plan 2 (3,000)
Cisco CallManager telephony with Unified Comms	Exchange Online Kiosk (10,000)
30 percent of workforce is factory-based	
Has Enterprise Agreement which includes Office	

As you can see there are quite a number of choices and scenarios available to organizations of all types and sizes. Making the correct choice involves identifying the requirements and which options address them.

Options to start your subscription

There are many ways to get started with an Office 365 subscription. Some of those ways include:

- Working with Microsoft on a license agreement (through a licensing reseller)
- Working with a Microsoft deployment partner
- Signing up for the service directly

Working with Microsoft on a license agreement (through a licensing reseller)

The chances are you are only working with Microsoft if you have a large set, or a combination of licenses, you need to purchase. An example of this would be if you are an enterprise customer seeking specific contract requirements and a combination of licenses, outside of Office 365, in a suite for your users. Specific contract requirements and suites of licenses are typically sold as **Enterprise Agreements (EA)**. The benefit of an EA is that it allows an organization to leverage a number of Microsoft products, for a single per seat cost. If you are an EA customer or plan to be one, the sign-up process is different. When you sign up for an EA, you will typically receive an e-mail with two options:

- The first option is to attach your license to an existing Office 365 trial account
- The second option is to create a new account with your licenses assigned

If you already purchased licenses in an existing account, it may be difficult for you to have Microsoft attach licenses to this account. Microsoft may ask you to recreate an account, in this scenario.

Working with a Microsoft deployment partner

If you are working with a Microsoft deployment partner, there is a good possibility the Microsoft deployment partner will be able to help you through this process. A Microsoft deployment partner has the ability to send you a customized link. This link can be a trial or a set of licenses to be purchased. The benefits of a Microsoft deployment partner sending you a link are twofold. The partner can help ensure you have the right licenses and the partner obtains benefits while being associated with your subscription. Those benefits include subscription notifications for changes/upgrades and there are financial benefits. The notifications/changes are of benefit, as the partner can work closely with your organization to ensure you are prepared for the upcoming changes. The financial benefits a partner receives are specifically related to the partner being an advisor for your subscription.

Signing up for the service directly

The last option is to sign up for the service directly. The chances are you are taking this approach if you are not signing an EA or are not working with a Microsoft deployment partner, and are planning to trial, or move to, this service on your own. Often at times, organizations sign up for the service ahead of working with a partner or Microsoft on licensing. If you have signed up for a trial service, but plan to work with a partner or Microsoft, it is recommended not to purchase licenses until you have requested their advise on how to proceed. The impacts of purchasing a license prior to engaging Microsoft or a partner can mean reallocating enabled accounts or a delay in how soon Microsoft can apply the EA licenses.

In all cases, we'll leverage the Office 365 admin portal `https://portal.microsoftonline.com/Admin` in a similar method. Before we get started with the Office 365 admin portal, we need to sign up for the service.

The sign-up process

We recently learned about the various subscription options. Now it's time to sign up for the service. In the following steps, we are simply going to sign up for a trial based subscription.

This will allow us the flexibility to choose how we add licenses in the near future:

1. To get started, let's head over to the Office 365 site. Simply go to www.
office365.com and find the **FREE TRIAL** link. You now have a decision
to make. Does the P plan fit your organization or do you have more than
50 users or plan to grow to more than 50 users in the near future? If your
answer is yes, then you need to head over to the E plan trial. In this example,
we will sign up for the E plan:

2. Once you have clicked on **FREE TRIAL** your next page will be a **Sign up**
page. This page will require you to enter your business information. You
will also be selecting your subscription name (your subscription name may
sometimes be referred to as your tenant name). This name is important for a
few reasons, as follows:

   ° Your SharePoint service has your subscription name (for example,
   pointbridgelab.sharepoint.com)

   ° It will be your default e-mail address or account name for your users,
   until you add your own vanity domains

   ° You will reference this name for support concerns

   ° Associating your Enterprise Agreement licenses to your subscription

The subscription name is important, but your long term users may never see
it, if you apply a vanity name. (a vanity domain is a simple name to mask a
more complex domain behind it.) During the sign up portion, you will have
an opportunity to check to see if your subscription name is free. If your name
is taken, try a few others until you find the name that fits your organization:

Email address is also a very important field. The e-mail address you add on this page will be the default e-mail address that receives messages from Office 365. In addition, subscription information and errors that may occur with your integration components will be sent to this address. Ensure you add an e-mail address that you plan to monitor.

3. After you have entered all of your information and proceeded to the next step, your subscription will now be created. You should be presented with a window that asks you to continue to your subscription. The screen will look similar to the following screenshot:

4. When you click on **Continue**, you will be redirected to your subscription. Within your subscription, you may notice that not all services are ready. Exchange and Lync are often ready immediately, but you may notice that it will take the SharePoint service around 15 to 60 minutes to become available:

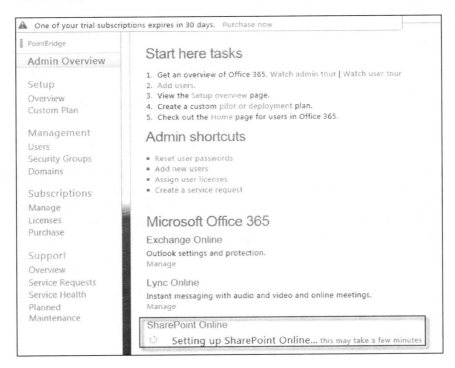

You can start to tour your subscription now, while waiting for SharePoint to be activated. You will not be able to make any configuration changes in SharePoint, until it is ready. If it takes the SharePoint service more than 24 hours to finish setting up, you should contact Office 365 support through a **Service Request**. Once the SharePoint service is set up, your sign up process is complete.

Summary

Office 365 offers many ways to subscribe and all sorts of licensing combinations. Whether you're a small business or an enterprise, you have a number of ways to get started. The good news is, you can start a trial subscription and always associate your long-term licenses to the trial, leveraging any method. We learned about the licensing available within the service, which should clarify how you proceed. By this time you should be deciding how these licenses fit your organization and whether you are going to sign up directly, work with a Microsoft Deployment Partner, or engage an Enterprise Agreement with Microsoft.

As we reflect on the sign-up process, you can see how simplified Microsoft designed the process; Microsoft focused on minimizing many decision points for a trial. The fact is, it is a trial, so why complicate the sign-up process more than it needs to be? Either way, in the end, your team managing and configuring the service will be required to do all of the tweaking and tuning, based on business and technical decisions made within the organization.

In conclusion, you should now be ready to start getting more familiar with the service, configuring it to your specifications, starting the integration process, and finally either migrating or starting to use the service full-time. Before your trial ends, you will need to obtain or assign, the licensing plan that best fits your subscription.

Now that we have established a subscription, in the next chapter we will focus on using the admin portal. We will also start to walk through some key initial configuration steps.

2
Getting Familiar with the Office 365 Admin Portal

Now that we have shown you how to sign up for Office 365, it's important to get familiar with the administration interface as it is the central control point for everything to do with your subscription.

In this chapter we will walk you through the high-level interface, adding a domain to your subscription, as well as dive deep into the administration sub-interfaces. Topics covered include:

- Logging in for the first time and adding your domain
- Navigating the Administration Overview interface
- The Exchange Online Administration interface

Logging in for the first time and adding your domain

To get to the administration interface, you will need to browse to `https://portal.microsoftonline.com` and log in with the credentials you chose during the sign-up process in *Chapter 1, Getting Started*:

The first step of utilizing Office 365 for your business requires that you add your domain (for example, `yourcompany.com`) in the portal. This is a necessary place to start as your domain will be used later in many aspects of the Admin Portal. To add your domain to Office 365, click on the **Domains** menu option on the left (see the following screenshot):

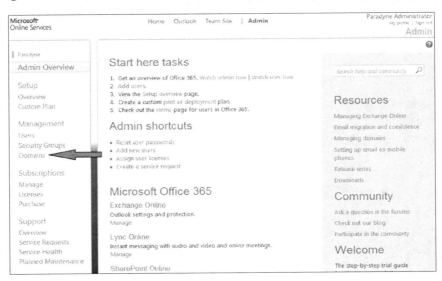

You will see that the tenant domain already exists (for example, `yourcompany.onmicrosoft.com`) in the listing. This domain cannot be removed, however after completing the next few steps, your Office 365 subscription will be set up in a way that the tenant domain will not be seen by your users.

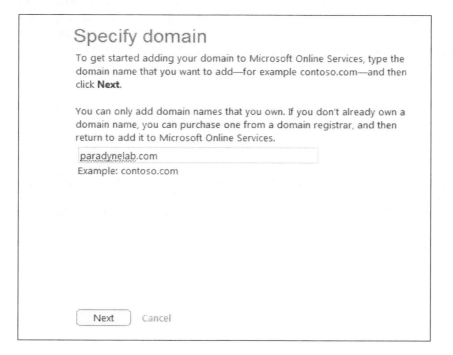

DNS requirements

Office 365 requires two key types of DNS records that are not supported by various domain name hosts or providers—TXT and SRV. Check with your domain host to ensure that they support the creation of those records within your domain name; otherwise you may need to change domain hosts before going further.

Click on **Add** to go to the next page where you will add your organization's domain names. Click on **Next**:

Specify domain

To get started adding your domain to Microsoft Online Services, type the domain name that you want to add—for example contoso.com—and then click **Next**.

You can only add domain names that you own. If you don't already own a domain name, you can purchase one from a domain registrar, and then return to add it to Microsoft Online Services.

paradynelab.com

Example: contoso.com

[Next]   Cancel

The domain wizard will then provide you with a list of popular domain name hosts which can display customized instructions. If your domain name host is not on the list, select **General instructions**:

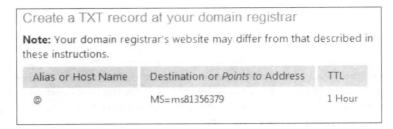

At this point, you will need to create the TXT record as instructed within your DNS provider's domain name control panel. The speed at which this DNS addition is visible by Office 365 depends on various factors—you may see it instantly or you may need to wait anywhere from 15 minutes to 72 hours to see the TXT record appear. Clicking on **Next** will begin the domain validation process, as shown in the following screenshot, to ensure that Office 365 can see the TXT record:

Now that the domain has been added, you need to specify the domain intent.

It is important that at this point, you do not check the **SharePoint Online** checkbox as it will grey out the other two options. This is due to the way that Office 365 handles domains specifically for SharePoint Online:

Once the domain has been added to Office 365, you will then be guided to configure the required DNS records to allow the domain to be used.

Before adding all the suggested DNS records to your domain name, it is important to check if any existing services are similar to the suggested DNS records. For example, if you are already using e-mail on `yourdomain.com` then you should not modify the MX record until you are ready (this will be addressed further in the book).

On adding the relevant DNS records in your host's domain name control panel and clicking on **Next** followed by **Finish**, you will then be brought back to the **Domains** listing where your domain should now be listed as **Verified**:

Now that your domain name has been added to Office 365, the final step is to mark it as the primary domain. This is achieved by clicking on your company name at the top-left of the Portal above **Admin Overview**:

Click on **Edit** and change the **Primary verified domain** field to be that of your company:

You have now successfully set up your domain within Office 365 and can begin using your subscription.

Navigating the Administration Overview interface

In this section of the chapter we will take you through the high-level administrative interface for Office 365. The interface is broken down into several sections:

- **Setup**
- **Management**
- **Subscriptions**
- **Support**

Setup

The **Setup** section assists you in beginning your journey with Office 365.

Overview

The **Overview** section provides you with general information about how to get started with your Office 365 subscription, as well as links to more information. We will cover most of this information throughout the rest of this book as it relates to migration and Exchange Online:

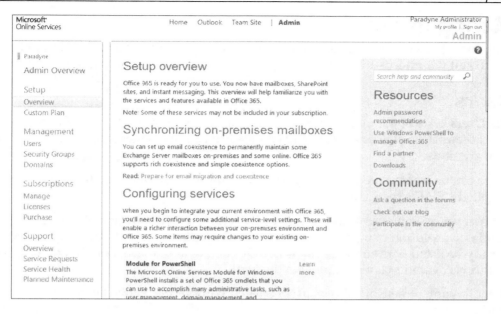

Custom Plan

The **Custom Plan** section provides you with a wizard that walks you through the "getting ready" steps for performing the migration to Office 365. Again, most of this will be covered in detail in the remainder of this book:

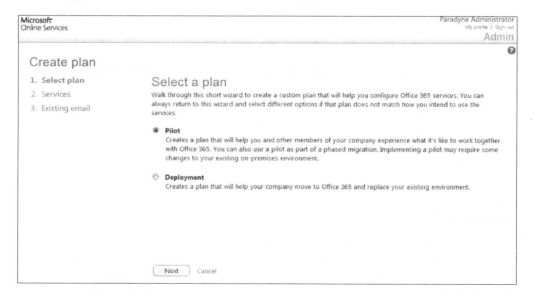

Management

The key objective of the management section is to configure (at a basic level) Office 365 to suit your needs by way of user, group, and domain administration.

Users

The **Users** page of the management interface allows you to create/modify/delete user accounts, as well as allocate and change licenses that are associated with accounts.

Users can be created on a one-by-one basis or imported in bulk by utilizing the supplied CSV file template.

If, however, you choose to utilize Active Directory synchronization either as a standalone solution or a part of Active Directory Federation Services, all users will already be listed here so the portal is merely used to assign licenses. Exactly how to do this is covered in later chapters in the book.

The following screenshot shows users created without the Active Directory synchronization:

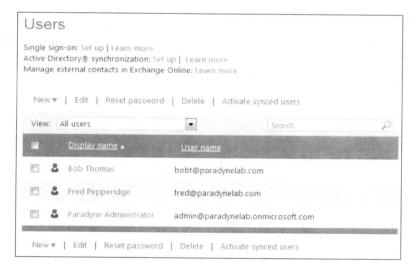

Security Groups

The **Security Groups** area of the admin portal is generally used to create groups for the single purpose of administration ease in SharePoint Online. The groups created in this section can only be used to control the groups' membership and cannot actually be mail enabled. This can only be achieved through the Exchange Online console which we will cover later in this chapter.

Similarly to users, if directory synchronization is enabled, it will bring across any groups from your Active Directory, as shown in the following screenshot. Security groups that have been synchronized across can also be turned into distribution groups within the Exchange Online control panel:

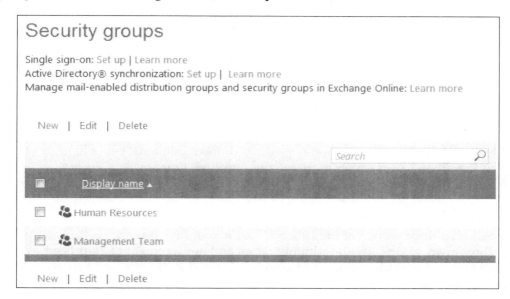

Domains

As you saw earlier in the chapter, the **Domains** interface is used to add internet-based domain names (for example, yourcompany.com) to Office 365:

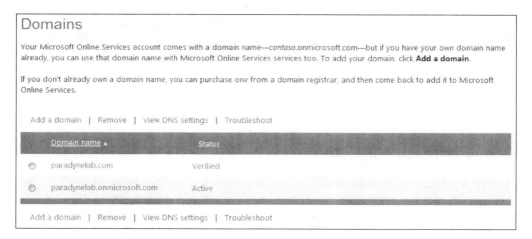

If you choose to utilize the public-facing website component, SharePoint Online, you will also need to add a separate record here (for example, www.yourcompany.com) and specify it for the sole purpose of SharePoint Online:

Specify domain services

Specify the services you'll use with your domain. Learn more

☐ Exchange Online
☐ Lync Online
☑ SharePoint Online

Additionally, if your organization requires additional domains, you will need to repeat the process seen earlier in this chapter for each domain.

Subscriptions

The **Subscriptions** section of the Office 365 administrative interface is broken up into three areas to simplify the administration and management of your licenses. From here, you may view your license and their purchase history, add partners, and purchase additional licenses.

Manage

By browsing to the **Manage** page, you can see the list of licenses allocated to your Office 365 environment:

Subscription	Quantity	Cost	Term end date
Microsoft Office 365 Trial (Plan E3)	25 user licenses	No cost	Expires 02 March 2012
Microsoft Office 365 Trial (Plan K2)	25 user licenses	No cost	Expires 02 March 2012

Selecting one of the subscriptions will display the billing address information, as well as the partner (if selected).

Different countries will have different relationships for their customers with Microsoft. In most countries you will be able to purchase your licenses directly from Microsoft, by clicking on the **Buy now** link on the page:

The **Buy now** option however is absent for countries such as Australia where licenses must be purchased through Telstra — the exclusive syndication partner for the country:

If you are working with a partner, it is important to add their information so that they may assist you in future with support. To do this, you will require their Microsoft partner ID which you can obtain by asking them:

After adding the partner information, you will see that this information shows up under the subscription details:

If you choose to work with a different partner in future you can easily change this information by going back to the screen, clicking on **Edit**, and entering the new partner's ID.

Licenses

The **Licenses** section is quite simple in its function—which is simply to display the number of licenses you are subscribed to and the number of them you have allocated:

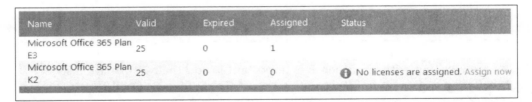

Purchase

The **Purchase** section of the subscription management is used to directly interact with the Microsoft commerce system to purchase additional licenses.

Again, this is different in some geographies, as shown in the following screenshot of the Office 365 trial tenant in the US version:

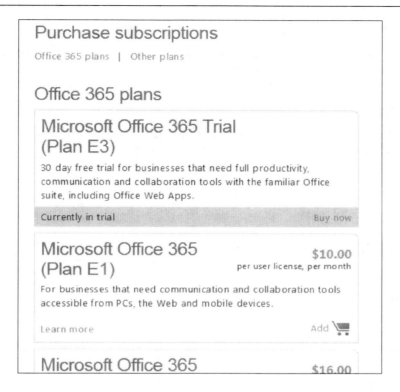

The following screenshot shows the Australian version of the page where purchasing licenses directly is not an option:

Support

The **Support** interface is the first point of call for any technical issues you may be having with your Office 365 subscription.

Overview

In the **Overview** page you will see a snapshot of all of the information and tools available to assist you with your Office 365 subscription:

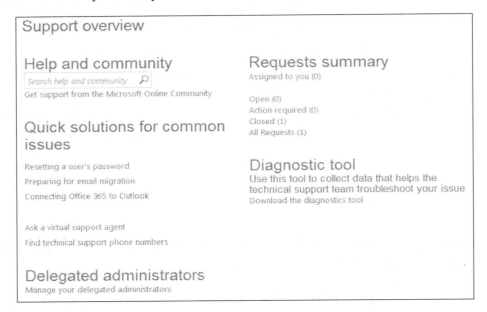

It is the first point any Office 365 administrator should visit to resolve any possible issues as it contains a wealth of information sourced from several areas such as Microsoft support and the Office 365 community.

Service Requests

If you require technical assistance and cannot find the answer in areas such as the Office 365 **Community** site or on the **Overview** page then submitting a service request is the next step. The issue identification process is very comprehensive, which allows the Office 365 support and escalation teams to deal with your issue in a much faster response time:

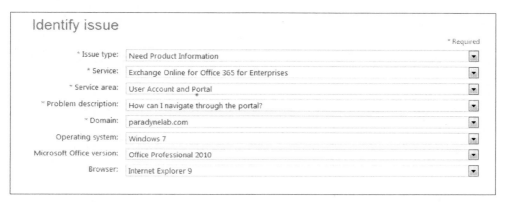

On submitting your service request, you will be able to modify its status at any time through the process and use it to interact with the support team.

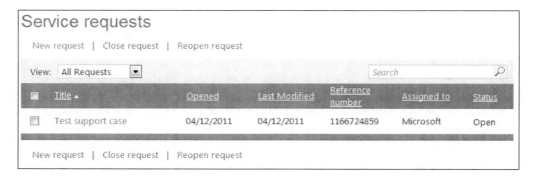

Service Health

If you believe that you are experiencing any form of service issue or degradation, the first place to check is the **Service health** page which displays a 7-day rolling history of any potential issues that may have occurred or are currently active:

Service health
Last refreshed: 16:00, 04 December 2011

Current status

Service	Today	Dec 3	Dec 2	Dec 1	Nov 30	Nov 29	Nov 28
Exchange Online ▲							
E-Mail and calendar access	✓	ℹ	✓	✓	✓	✓	✓
E-Mail timely delivery	✓	✓	✓	✓	✓	✓	✓
Management and Provisioning	✓	✓	✓	✓	✓	✓	✓
Sign-in	✓	✓	✓	✓	✓	✓	✓
Identity Service ▼	✓	✓	✓	✓	✓	✓	✓
Lync Online ▲							
All Features	✓	✓	✓	✓	✓	✓	✓
Audio and Video	✓	✓	✓	✓	✓	✓	✓
Dial-In Conferencing	✓	✓	✓	✓	✓	✓	✓
Federation	✓	✓	✓	✓	✓	✓	✓
Instant Messaging	✓	✓	✓	✓	✓	✓	✓
Management and Provisioning	✓	✓	✓	✓	✓	✓	✓
Online Meetings	✓	✓	✓	✓	✓	✓	✓
Presence	✓	✓	✓	✓	✓	✓	✓
Sign-In	✓	✓	✓	✓	ℹ	✓	✓
Microsoft Online Portal ▲							
Administration	✓	✓	ℹ	ℹ	ℹ	ℹ	ℹ

Planned Maintenance

Being aware of what maintenance is scheduled allows you, as an Office 365 administrator, to better serve your organization by understanding the potential impact to their productivity. As administrators you are even able to see the process of any maintenance that is scheduled, in progress or completed simply by clicking on the **Planned Maintenance** menu item:

Planned maintenance
Last refreshed: 16:03, 04 December 2011

Upcoming maintenance

Service	Date and time	Status	Details
Exchange Online	23 Nov 2011 05:00	In progress	Server-side certificates used to encrypt HTTP traffic from clients are being updated to refresh expiration dates. No customer action is required and no customer impact is expected.
Lync Online	30 Nov 2011 02:00	In progress	Lync Online team is currently deploying CU4 into the North American environments. Expected Impact - There is no significant impact expected on Lync or other services.. Typically the impact will be a disconnect followed by an automatic reconnect, but for conference disconnects users will have to rejoin manually. The users will also see resiliency mode or unknown presence for 10 minutes.

Exchange Online administration interface

Delving deeper into the Exchange Online administration interface is possible by clicking on **Manage** under **Exchange Online** in the **Admin Overview** page:

This will open a new tab within your browser and provide you with much more granular access to the interface.

While a great many features and functions are available through the web-based Exchange Online administration interface, a lot of functions are only available through PowerShell which will be covered later in the book.

Users & Groups

In the **Users & Groups** section of Exchange Online management, you have the ability to:

- Create user mailboxes
- Modify properties of user mailboxes
- Create room mailboxes (for example, meeting rooms)
- Create distribution groups or mail enabled security groups
- External contacts
- Perform mailbox migrations from Exchange 2010, 2007, 2003, and IMAP mail systems

Roles & Auditing

In the **Roles & Auditing** section of the Exchange Online management you have the ability to:

- Define administrator roles and permission levels
- Define the level of self-administration available to end users
- Run auditing reports for:
    - Non-owner mailbox access
    - Litigation hold
    - Administration role group
- Export mailbox audit logs
- Export administrator audit logs

Mail Control

The **Mail Control** area of Exchange Online allows Office 365 administrators to take control of the mail flow at a granular level both external to/from their organization, as well as internally.

From this interface, the administrators are able to:

- Define rules to control the mail flow within the organization
- Configure IP safe listing, message tracing (external), and e-mail policies
- Define journaling rules for e-mail retention and archival strategy
- Run delivery reports

Phone & Voice

Moving beyond the mailbox and onto both mobile devices and unified messaging, Exchange Online can become the cornerstone of organizational communications.

Despite being in the cloud, customers are able to connect their IP telephony systems (such as Lync Server 2010, Cisco CallManager, Avaya IP Office, and most other SIP-compliant systems) to Exchange Online. This allows for organizations to have a single system for mail, be it voicemail or e-mail (a.k.a. unified messaging).

The two key features that facilitate this functionality are:

- **Unified Messaging Dial Plans** which ensure that both Exchange Online and your IP phone system can translate phone numbers to e-mail addresses
- **Unified Messaging IP Gateways** which allow the conversation between Exchange Online and the IP phone system to speak in the first place

The second component of the **Phone & Voice** menu is the ability to control and manage how mobile devices work with Office 365.

Mobile devices that include the ActiveSync protocol can be managed in great detail, allowing you to:

- Quarantine devices and set appropriate rules and notifications
- Control which devices can connect to Exchange Online (for example, restrict either operating systems such as Android or manufacturers such as HTC)
- Create security policies to control and restrict mobile access to Exchange Online, such as requiring PIN security and specifying how many failed attempts before performing a remote wipe of the device

Summary

In this chapter we showed you how to find your way around Office 365 and the Exchange Online administrative interface. We also showed you how to start customizing Office 365 by adding your own domain to the environment. From here, you should now have the knowledge and tools to begin planning your migration to Exchange Online.

In the next chapter, we will discuss the integration options available when using the Office 365 for Small Businesses and Professionals plan.

3
Integration Options for Small Businesses and Professionals

For many small businesses, moving to the cloud can be a daunting task and can also be a significant change in the way they operate on a daily basis. Decisions need to be made around whether to have a mixture of on-premise and cloud services or to simply go with "all in". Certain advanced features of Exchange Online and PowerShell are often neglected by small businesses due to their perceived complexity. In this chapter we will aim to simplify this by providing you with information on:

- Business scenarios
- Working with a server
- Managing user accounts
- Working with PowerShell

Business scenarios

Organizations around the world come in a variety of shapes and sizes. As Office 365 for Small Businesses and Professionals is limited to 50 users and does not support Directory Synchronization, customers are limited in what choices they can make to integrate with on-premise solutions.

For many small businesses that are looking to move to Office 365 they may be doing so for a variety of reasons.

Ageing server

IT is generally relegated to business support and rarely seen as a revenue generator, with small businesses holding on to their servers as long as possible. As such they are usually reluctant to spend a portion of their capital to fund another depreciating asset. For this reason, Office 365 becomes an attractive option as there is no capital outlay to start using the service.

Remote workforce

With the ready availability of mobile broadband and the decreasing cost of portable devices such as laptops and tablets, many organizations are finding that their staff are spending more time out on the road or working from home.

Accessing e-mails, files, and applications from a central office location through a VPN can often be a hindrance to remote workers if the server is unavailable for various reasons (office Internet connectivity, server issues, and so on). Users need the flexibility of being able to access their content wherever they are and on whatever device they may be using.

For these small businesses, moving to Office 365 alleviates many challenges and potential issues that may affect the business productivity, and ultimately the profitability.

Staff expansion

When organizations expand, the IT requirements can often get in the way. Traditionally businesses would need to purchase (on top of hardware) additional server licenses, and obtain the services of an IT professional to connect and configure systems.

Office 365 greatly simplifies this by reducing the requirements to the procurement of hardware and a new user subscription; everything else can be done by the user.

Working with a server

When moving to Office 365, customers face the question—do I still need my server? For many, the requirement to continue using a server is negated based on the functionality that Office 365 provides and as such they are able to remove their server after their migration is complete.

However, some businesses may still require the services of an on-premise server for a variety of reasons such as file systems, databases, and line of business applications.

In the latter case, a business would now be faced with the challenge of maintaining two disparate systems (being their server and Office 365).

Generally a business can maintain a single set of usernames through the implementation of Directory Synchronization. However, this is not available with Office 365 for Small Businesses and Professionals. This applies to businesses running:

- Windows Server 2003
- Windows Server 2008
- Small Business Server 2003
- Small Business Server 2008
- Small Business Server 2011 Standard

In the case of a business running any of these server solutions, the recommendation would be to purchase the Office 365 for Enterprise subscription in order to utilize Directory Synchronization. The integration options for these server solutions are covered in *Chapter 4, Integration Options for Enterprises*.

However, if a business can tolerate managing two separate sets of usernames, there is a saving grace with a variety of third-party password synchronization solutions available (for example, MessageOps and SADA Systems). This allows businesses to at least keep passwords the same for the users, both on the server and within Office 365, facilitating an improved user experience.

Small Business Server 2011 Essentials

Microsoft Small Business Server 2011 Essentials (SBS2011E) is the first server solution to natively support Office 365 through the Integration Module.

By utilizing this server solution and module, businesses can have a seamless user management experience between the on-premise server and Office 365.

It is important to note that the user limitation of SBS2011E is 25, whereas Office 365 for Small Businesses and Professionals has a 50 user limitation.

Connecting your Small Business Server 2011 Essentials to Office 365

Before being able to manage Office 365 through the SBS2011E Dashboard, the Office 365 Integration Module must be installed (it's a free download from Microsoft).

 You may need to reboot your server as part of the installation.

After completing the installation there will now be a **Set up Microsoft Office 365 Integration** task, as shown in the following screenshot:

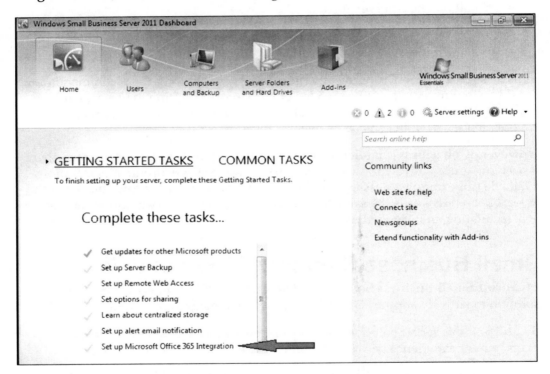

As we have already signed up for an Office 365 subscription, we can select this option and move on to provisioning our service:

We must now enter the username and password of an account that is used to administer Office 365:

 It is recommended that you do not use your own account for this and instead use the provided **admin** account, as your password may change which will stop the integration from working.

At this point, you will be asked to adhere to the Office 365 strong password policy:

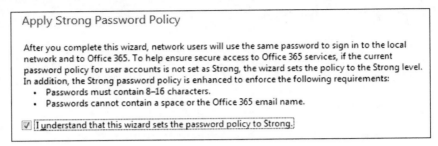

The server will then take a few moments while it connects to Office 365 and verifies your credentials:

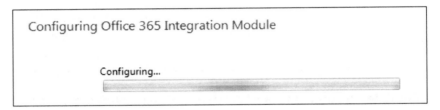

On completion of the module configuration, the server will need to be restarted in order to show up on the Small Business Server Dashboard:

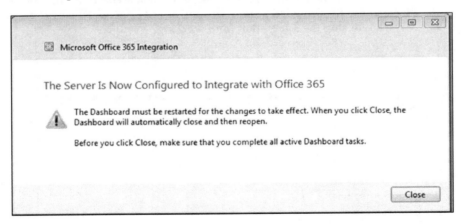

On rebooting, you should now see the **Office 365** icon appear in the Dashboard, as shown in the following screenshot:

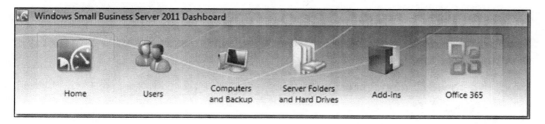

Clicking on the **Office 365** icon will take you to the Office 365 interface which obtains information about your subscription:

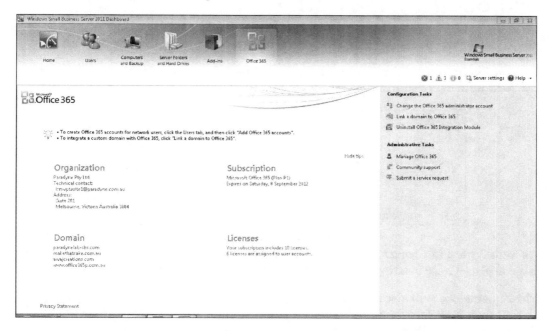

As we have already verified the domain in the previous chapters, we will now see it displayed under the **Domain** section on the screen without having to follow the **Link a domain to Office 365** process.

Managing user accounts

There are three options available to Office 365 administrators for managing user accounts. These are:

- Microsoft Online Portal
- SBS2011E Dashboard
- Windows PowerShell

Microsoft Online Portal

To manage users via the Microsoft Online Portal the first step is to log in to `http://portal.microsoftonline.com` with your administrative credentials.

On logging in to the Admin interface, you will be able to create new users by using the **Add new users** shortcut or by clicking on the **Users** menu under **Management**:

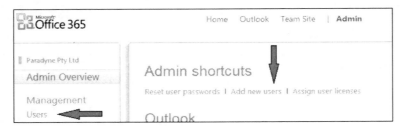

As highlighted in *Chapter 2, Getting Familiar with the Office 365 Admin Portal*, the **Users** page is also where existing users can be modified and deleted.

Most businesses will also require e-mail groups (known as Distribution Groups) so that they may receive e-mails sent to generic e-mail addresses and distribute them amongst multiple users. An example of a generic e-mail ID would be `sales@yourdomain.com`; an e-mail sent to this ID is received by all the sales people. This can also be used for departmental e-mail distribution; for example, an e-mail sent to `finance@yourdomain.com` goes to all members of the finance team.

This functionality can be administered by accessing the **Distribution groups** shortcut on the front page:

Clicking on this shortcut, you will be taken to the **Exchange Control Panel (ECP)** to work with Distribution Groups.

SBS2011E Dashboard

If you have previously created accounts on Small Business Server 2011 Essentials, you can use the server dashboard to provision these accounts for Office 365 and begin to manage them.

As you can see in the following screenshot, the server is able to query Office 365 directly. You can see that no accounts have been provisioned. The first step is to assign an Office 365 account. This involves only a few mouse clicks to complete:

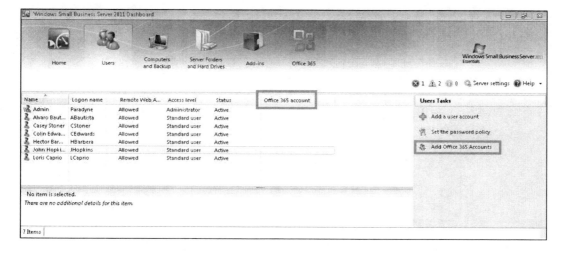

At this point we are able to choose if we want to create a new Office 365 account or use an existing account that may have been created previously. For demonstrative purposes, we will assume that no accounts have been created in your Office 365 environment yet. On making the selection to create a new Office 365 account you will need to specify the e-mail address that is to be used:

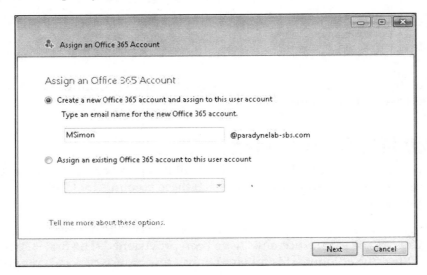

This process will then run PowerShell cmdlets, behind the scenes, to create an account and link it to the account in SBS2011e:

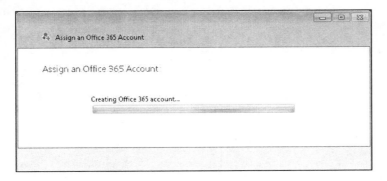

One of the key features of the Office 365 Integration Module for Small Business Server 2011 Essentials is the built-in password synchronization functionality. To complete the user creation process within Office 365, you will need to change the user's Windows password so that it can perform the initial password synchronization with Office 365:

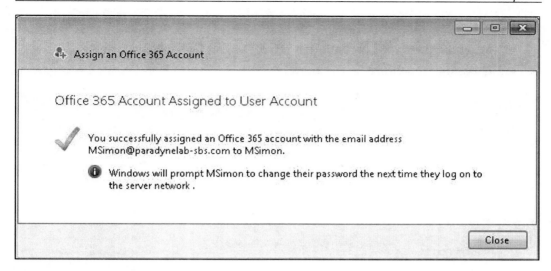

After completing the account provisioning process, you will see that the Office 365 account is now connected to the SBS2011e account:

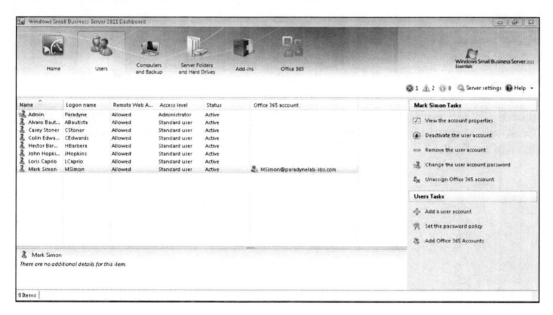

From this point, you have the option to manage the account in one of two ways:

- Reset the password on both, the SBS2011e and Office 365 accounts
- Un-assign the Office 365 account

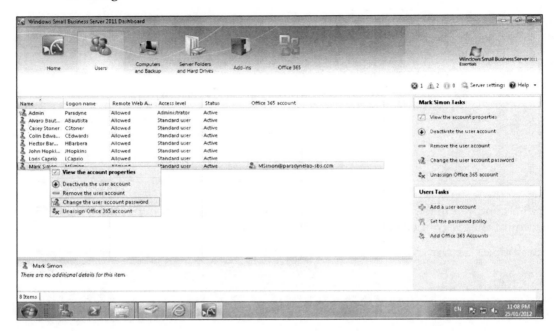

In order to add multiple Office 365 accounts and connect them to existing Windows users, you simply need to highlight the relevant accounts and follow the same process as above:

When the process is completed a slightly different version of the success screen is shown (see the following screenshot):

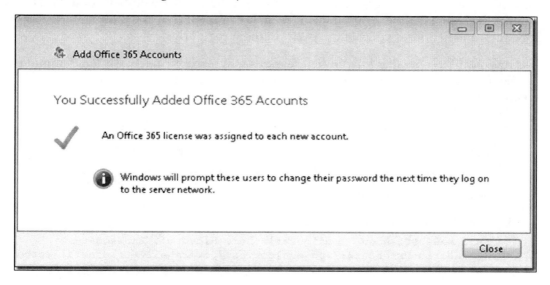

Windows PowerShell

Using PowerShell with Office 365 is broken up into two forms of administration:

- General Office 365 administration
- Exchange Online advanced administration

Connecting to Windows PowerShell for Office 365 requires the installation of the Microsoft Online Services Sign-in Assistant in order to adequately pass credentials to Office 365. Most of the functions that are usually performed under Windows PowerShell for Office 365 can be performed through the Microsoft Online Portal: therefore, this is not really applicable for small businesses.

Working with PowerShell

There are numerous Exchange Online functions that can only be performed through PowerShell. These are:

- Setting mailbox permissions
- Creating a shared mailbox
- Allowing users to send e-mails on behalf of other users

Any Windows 7 computer is capable of running Windows PowerShell commands against Exchange Online. You can also create PowerShell scripts to automate functions and actions if you plan to perform them regularly.

It is important to note that PowerShell sessions may become inactive after 15 minutes of idle time, so make sure you know what commands you need to run before creating the connection.

Connecting to Exchange Online with PowerShell involves a few steps:

1. Load Windows PowerShell (search for it through the **Start** menu).

2. Specify your Office 365 administrative credentials as follows:

    ```
    $cred = Get-Credential
    ```

3. Establish a new PowerShell session with the Exchange Online interface:

    ```
    $s = New-PSSession -ConfigurationName Microsoft.Exchange
    -ConnectionUri https://ps.outlook.com/powershell -Credential $cred
    -Authentication Basic -AllowRedirection
    ```

4. Import the Exchange Online PowerShell cmdlets:

    ```
    $importresults = Import-PSSession $s
    ```

5. Now you are ready to begin running commands to perform your desired functions:

```
Get-PSSession
```

PowerShell cmdlets follow this path:

- Verb
- Noun
- Required parameters, inputs and variables

The following table shows an example cmdlet to obtain the mailbox size for a single user:

Verb	Noun	Parameter	Input	Pipe	Parameter	Variable
Add	Mailbox Statistics	-Identity	john@ paradynelab-sbs.com	|	Select	total itemsize

The following table shows an example cmdlet to grant access to a mailbox:

Verb	Noun	Parameter	Input	Parameter	Variable	Parameter	Input
Add	Mailbox Per mission	-Identity	john@ paradyne lab-sbs. com	-Access Right	Full access	User	sarah@ paradyne lab-sbs. com

As you work with the the Exchange Online control panel (the web-based admin interface), there will be various functions or actions you want to perform that are simply not possible. Rest assured, in most cases these can actually be done through PowerShell.

Summary

In this chapter we saw some of the options available for integrating your existing small business environment with Office 365, as well as managing your user accounts.

As has been demonstrated, the different methods available, range in complexity and are suitable based on your comfort levels.

In the next chapter, we will see how to prepare for a Simple Migration from an existing mail platform to Exchange Online.

4
Integration Options for Enterprises

Moving to the cloud for some of the services you provide today is a major shift in how you manage both your infrastructure and users. The key item to focus on when moving to the cloud is what type of experience you choose to provide your users with, whether it's migrating from Exchange and preventing a new download of cached mail, or seamlessly authenticating from SharePoint Online while navigating to SharePoint on-premise. To provide this experience, you need to enable some of the core integration options provided by Microsoft Online. The topics covered in this chapter include:

- Directory Synchronization
- Active Directory Federation Services (ADFS)
- Exchange Hybrid
- Non-Exchange messaging systems

Directory Synchronization

Directory Synchronization allows organizations with an Active Directory (AD) environment to synchronize the AD users and groups to an Office 365 subscription. The Directory Synchronization tool provided by Microsoft can only synchronize a single AD forest and within this single forest, all the domains are synchronized.

Microsoft offers two versions of the Directory Synchronization software. The 32-bit version, which was the first version released, followed by the 64-bit version. Currently these two versions are in feature parity. The 32-bit version is based on Microsoft's **Identity Lifecycle Manager 2007 (ILM)** and the 64-bit version is based on Microsoft's **Forefront Identity Manager 2010 (FIM)**.

Once you deploy Directory Synchronization in your environment, you should consider this server to be a permanent addition to your environment. Microsoft will likely phase out the 32-bit version of the Directory Synchronization software, so it's highly recommended that you deploy the 64-bit version, as we would expect additional synchronization features to be released in the 64-bit version only.

There are many benefits for synchronizing your AD environment to Office 365. These benefits include the following:

- Enabling a unified address book
- Providing detailed address entries
- Simplifying the provisioning and object management process
- Maintaining a consistent set of groups

Enabling a unified address book

When you plan a migration to Exchange Online, you may be planning for a pilot migration or even a staged migration approach. Maintaining a single address book across the messaging systems will be critical. This single address book will simplify the overall communications.

Directory Synchronization allows the Outlook users to see on-premise mailboxes. When an Exchange Online user sends an e-mail to an on-premise user, Exchange detects that the mailbox or license for that user does not exist and then routes the mail to the on-premise mailbox. Setting the primary e-mail domain in Exchange Online to "Shared" is a critical step for this to be successful. We will learn more about this in *Chapter 7, Preparing for a Hybrid Deployment and Migration*. The scenario is the same for an e-mail from on-premise to Exchange Online; however, in this case the mailbox has the forwarder or target address of a service domain within Exchange Online.

Providing detailed address entries

At a minimum, Directory Synchronization requires the following attributes:

- `cn`
- `member` (applies only to groups)
- `samAccountName` (applies only to users)
- `alias` (applies only to groups and contacts)
- `displayName` (for groups with a `mail` or a `proxyAddresses` attribute populated)

The above attributes do not provide a great user experience for users leveraging any of the Office 365 services. Office 365 allows you to synchronize so much more. As an example, you can synchronize the first names, last names, e-mail addresses, office locations, manager, phone numbers, and so on. If you have Exchange on-premise you likely have most of these attributes filled in. These attributes offer a great benefit for maintaining a simplified address book in Exchange and a more complete directory in SharePoint Online.

If you have another messaging system such as Lotus Notes or GroupWise, then you may not have the earlier mentioned attributes filled in. In order to provide a rich user experience, it's highly recommended that you populate these attributes. Many third-party migration tools will help you in organizing and populating this information. If you maintain this information in an external system (for example, an HR system), you may want to consider leveraging an identity management solution to keep your AD and external system in sync.

To learn more about which attributes are synchronized, review the list provided by Microsoft at `http://support.microsoft.com/kb/2256198`.

Simplifying the provisioning and object management process

By default, the Directory Synchronization process runs every three hours. After the first run, the synchronization process looks for changes within the environment. These changes can consist of attribute changes (for example, manager or title change) or they can consist of additions/deletions within the environment.

The advantage of Directory Synchronization is to prevent organizations from having to manage multiple directories. When you maintain multiple directories, you can cause a significant disconnect in object information. This can also be a security risk to most organizations, as you may be leaving access open to individuals that should no longer have it.

As Directory Synchronization enforces changes within Office 365, during synchronization, you can simplify your provisioning process. As an example, when you want to provision a user, you add them to AD as you normally would. Once you add them to AD, you then license them for the services they need in Office 365 after synchronization. It's even more simplified when you de-provision a user. When de-provisioning a user, all that is required is either disabling or removing their account within your AD environment. Once you remove their account in AD, their license will then free up in Office 365 on the next synchronization and their mailbox will be removed.

Organizations that leverage an existing identity management solution or plan to leverage one in the future can take advantage of the simplified provisioning options from Microsoft Office 365. Here is an example of a provisioning process you might consider:

1. Provision a user in your HR system.
2. Your identity management solution creates the account(s) in AD.
3. The identity management solution forces an Office 365 directory synchronization manually (to be executed on the Directory Synchronization server, if this is not possible, wait for 3 hours).
4. Run a PowerShell command to provision a license for the user in Office 365.

Maintaining a consistent set of groups

Managing groups apart from AD could be challenging, especially if these groups maintain security for a SharePoint site or a distribution list for companywide e-mails. Directory Synchronization synchronizes both the security groups and the distribution lists. The only difference between these groups within Office 365 is that the distribution lists also have a display name and an e-mail address. It is possible to have a security group serve as both a security group and distribution list.

Security groups can only be leveraged within SharePoint Online, unless the security group is mail-enabled. It's highly recommended that you continue to maintain security groups within AD; however your strategy to leverage SharePoint groups or security groups will depend on your approach for SharePoint Online. There are many advantages to leveraging security groups within SharePoint. The biggest advantage may come with a Hybrid deployment of SharePoint Online, while providing a seamless transition from Exchange Online to on-premise.

Distribution lists, on the other hand, have different advantages and disadvantages for being leveraged in AD.

Some of the common advantages of distribution list management in AD are as follows:

- Continue to manage your on-premise process for groups/lists
- Simplified helpdesk management of distribution lists
- Maintain your existing groups/ lists already established within AD
- In Hybrid mode, leverage the same lists for both online and on-premise users

Some of the common disadvantages of distribution list management in AD are as follows:

- Users cannot directly modify distribution lists, unless the list was created in Office 365 or the authority belongs to Office 365, for that group

- Group membership changes will take up to 3 hours, while waiting for directory synchronization

An example of how you may position Directory Synchronization in your environment is shown in the following diagram:

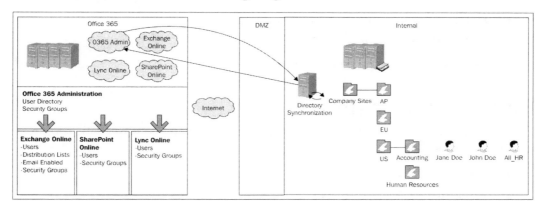

Active Directory Federation Services (ADFS)

With Office 365, Microsoft offers a single account sign-on experience, or single sign-on. Microsoft leverages **Active Directory Federation Service 2.0 (ADFS)** to provide this single sign-on experience. ADFS enables organizations to connect their existing Active Directory (AD) forest to Microsoft's federation infrastructure, creating a secure trust relationship with Microsoft. Once your organization is connected to this service, you can then allow your users to log on to the Office 365 services you provide, with their Active Directory credentials. There are many benefits for organizations providing this type of access. These benefits include:

- A simplified logon experience

- Less confusion versus maintaining multiple accounts/passwords

- Business control to quickly disable access to AD accounts when an employee leaves the organization

- AD policy adherence defined by the business (for example, password complexities, password attempt limits, and so on)

- Internal/External logon restrictions (for example, allowing users to only connect to the service while on the corporate networks, versus connecting outside the corporate network without a VPN)
- Enhanced security (for example, two-factor authentication)
- Ability to provide simplified logons for all ADFS services

In order to deploy ADFS within your environment, there are some initial areas to consider:

- Base requirements
- Database requirements
- Authentication strategy
- Infrastructure design considerations

Base requirements

The following are some of the base requirements you should consider. These base requirements include:

- Active Directory
- Windows 2003, 2008, or 2008 R2 domain controllers
- Publicly routable User Principal Name (UPN) (for example, a valid UPN is `%username%@domain.com`, not `domain\%username%`)

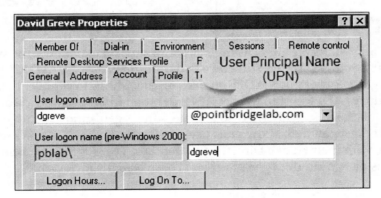

Many organizations have their users log on as `domain\%username%`, which has been a standard practice since the first logon methods, when domains were introduced in the Windows NT days. Changing to this standard is not difficult, but it will be an important communication/training for your end users when they leverage the Office 365 service. You do not need to change the computer logon to a UPN logon, just the logon to Office 365 services. If you do not leverage a publicly routable UPN in AD, you can simply add one by following these steps:

1. Go to **Active Directory Domains and Trusts**.

2. Go to **Properties** of Domains and Trust.

3. On the **UPN Suffixes** tab, add the UPN you plan to register for Office 365.

4. Now update the users for whom you would like to have this UPN.

It's also important to leverage a UPN that closely matches the user's e-mail address. The reason why this is important is that a UPN looks like an e-mail address and by providing this to your users, you may cause confusion if it's a different address. There are also some other complexities to services such as Lync, when leveraging a different UPN for a user's logon versus their e-mail address.

Single ADFS farm versus multiple farms

When you deploy ADFS, you essentially create a single ADFS farm. An **ADFS farm** is a set of ADFS servers that communicate to a single database source. When you assign a UPN to a user, they can only authenticate to one ADFS farm. Most organizations will leverage a single farm; however, you may consider multiple farms if you leverage multiple UPNs and you choose to provide local authentication to regional areas that connect to the same Active Directory environment.

You also need to plan to deploy an Office 365 Directory Synchronization server. This service is a key requirement for ADFS. The Directory Synchronization server updates your Office 365 subscription with all of the federated versus non-federated accounts. This is important, so the service knows not to allow a logon without approval from your Active Directory environment.

Database requirements

In addition to the base requirements, ADFS also requires a database server to attach to. The out of the box configuration is ready to attach to a **Windows Internal Database (WID.)** WID is basically a SQL Express deployment within Windows.

For most base deployments, WID is acceptable. WID has the following limitations:

- WID does not tolerate high latency connections (you cannot deploy multiple ADFS servers in a single ADFS farm and span it across slow WAN links)
- WID can only support up to five ADFS internal servers
- Only one ADFS internal server will be considered the master read/write server

If you plan to span ADFS across multiple sites with slow connections, or you plan to deploy more than five servers, you may want to consider a SQL deployment to support the ADFS servers.

Authentication strategy

Another requirement for ADFS is planning out your authentication strategy. The major fact you need to know about ADFS is how it routes the user to the ADFS servers. Today, DNS is primarily used to refer the connecting client to the appropriate ADFS server. All users have to log on to the service with a UPN. As mentioned earlier it looks similar to `%username%@domain.com` and the user's logon domain is `companydomain.com`. As DNS is used, you are somewhat limited on how you leverage ADFS. The following diagram shows an example demonstrating the first few steps of authentication:

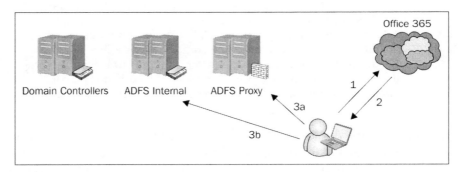

The first step is for the user to request access to the service. Office 365 then determines if the user is an ADFS or a non-ADFS user, based on UPN. If the user is an ADFS user, the user is then referred to an address set up within the service. As an example, it may be `sts.domain.com` (based on the user's UPN.) The end user then does a DNS lookup for the location of that server (the `STS DNS A` record part.) If the end user is outside the network (for example, public IP outside the internal network where ADFS is located), the user will likely get a public IP address for the ADFS proxy servers, which will securely traverse to the internal AD infrastructure (see path *3a*, in the preceding diagram). If the end user is within the internal private routable network on the same network as the ADFS internal server, the user will receive the internal IP address for the ADFS internal servers.

The primary limitation with this setup, for all users leveraging the UPN as `@domain.com`, is that you can only have one DNS record to refer the user to a proxy or internal ADFS server. This creates challenges for those companies looking to globally distribute ADFS for redundancy or performance reasons.

For those companies looking for redundancy or local authentication performance, there are some options. The companies that want to maintain the same UPN for all users, but need to provide global redundancy, can deploy a DNS solution that enables the capability to load the balance information between sites. This is based on the location of the user, availability of the services, and general performance of the servers. **F5** (`http://www.f5.com/solutions/availability/global-load-balancing/`) is one example of a great option to enable this capability. With a solution from F5, you can deploy an ADFS server to each of your sites dedicated to ADFS, and then rely on the F5 DNS service to direct your users to the appropriate servers.

 Review the ADFS Office 365 guides from Microsoft, when scaling ADFS servers.

If you are required, or have the ability to manage multiple UPNs, you have the option to deliver users to a specific site, based on their UPN. The following diagram shows an example of how this would work:

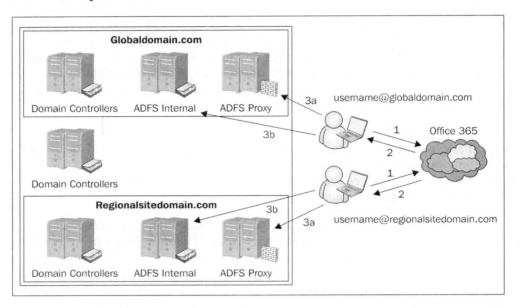

Infrastructure design considerations

Many organizations have various operating requirements or **Service-level Agreements (SLA)** when deploying certain types of service within their infrastructure. In most organizations, e-mailing is considered a mission critical service for their end users. With that, ADFS offers organizations a great amount of deployment options to support various internal SLAs for the servers hosted by that organization. These requirements often include:

- Base infrastructure
- Base infrastructure with redundancy
- Base infrastructure with redundancy and a disaster recovery site
- Base global infrastructure to support local regional logons

Let's review what these deployments may look like in your organization.

Base infrastructure

At the core of it, there are minimum infrastructure requirements to support ADFS within an organization. These minimum requirements include:

- ADFS internal server
- ADFS proxy server
- Directory Synchronization server

The following diagram shows an example of a base infrastructure:

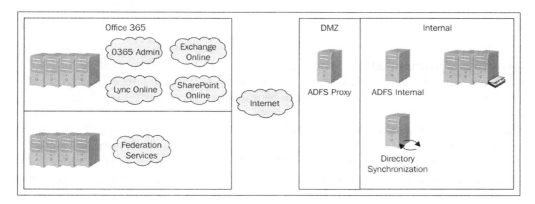

Base infrastructure with redundancy

If the ADFS internal server or ADFS proxy server were to go down, your users would not be able to authenticate to the Office 365 service. What this means is, your users will not be able to connect to read e-mails online or in an active state. To most organizations, this is unacceptable. To fulfill a base infrastructure with localized redundancy, you may consider the following items:

- ADFS Internal
    - ° Single primary internal server
    - ° Redundant internal server
    - ° Managed by software or hardware load balancing
- ADFS Proxy
    - ° Redundant proxy servers
    - ° Managed by software or hardware load balancing
- Directory Synchronization server

The following diagram shows an example of a base infrastructure with redundancy:

Now you are probably asking, why is there not a redundant Directory Synchronization server? Directory synchronization only occurs every 3 hours, out of the box. The purpose of directory synchronization is to ensure that Office 365 has the most recent account information from your local AD environment. If this server was to go down, your loss would only be no updates to Office 365. This server does not need to be up for users to log on (as long as the user's account has already been synchronized.) Arguably, you could build a standby server for Directory Synchronization, but you could also rebuild this server in a few hours, if you have a virtual or another readily available server. Your downtime would be pretty limited, if you have the options mentioned above.

Base infrastructure with redundancy and a disaster recovery site

Many organizations today require disaster recovery sites for all critical services. These disaster recovery sites often mirror their data centers, in the event a core service goes down. Adding a disaster recovery site adds complexity to the base deployment of the Office 365 infrastructure.

The ADFS internal and ADFS proxy servers have a single dependency of a Directory Synchronization server to enable users for authentication. When you install ADFS, you are required to attach it to a database server. The standard configuration for a base ADFS installation is to attach it to WID; however, when you plan to span ADFS across multiple sites, you may need to consider a SQL deployment. To fulfill a base infrastructure with localized redundancy and a disaster recovery site, you may consider the following items:

- ADFS Internal
  - ○ Single primary internal server
  - ○ Redundant internal server
  - ○ Managed by software or hardware load balancing
  - ○ Communications with a SQL Cluster
  - ○ Single or dual internal server at the **Disaster Recovery (DR)** site

- ADFS Proxy
  - ○ Redundant proxy servers
  - ○ Managed by software or hardware load balancing
  - ○ Single or dual proxy server at the DR site

- SQL Cluster
  - ○ Two SQL servers at the primary site, supported by Windows Clustering
  - ○ Single or dual SQL servers at the DR site, leveraging geo-clustering, replication, or mirroring

- Directory Synchronization server

The following diagram shows an example of a base infrastructure with redundancy:

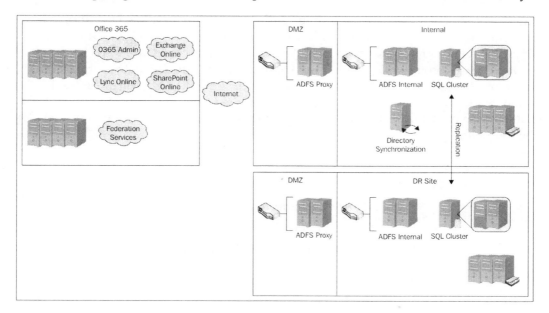

There are a few important things to note in order to support this type of configuration. To start, your SQL environment needs to be able to synchronize the changes frequently and read/write will have to take place, to the SQL DB, once the ADFS servers are active in the DR site. Another consideration is how you plan to fail over to the DR site. Consider leveraging a solution that can perform failover for a DNS record. You may deploy a DNS failover solution or an infrastructure solution that enables failover for data centers.

Base global infrastructure to support local regional logons

Some organizations operate independently based on sites or regions, but support the same infrastructure throughout. These organizations may also manage their own existing AD domains and messaging infrastructure. In some cases, it may be necessary to deploy independent ADFS environments, to support local management and authentication for those sites.

This may come in two forms—a redundant ADFS deployment covering multiple sites or independent ADFS farms at each site. Redundancy for an ADFS farm allows you to use a single UPN across all of these sites; however, having redundancy does not guarantee that you can direct users to the appropriate site. To accomplish this, you would need to have a load balancer that can sense where the user is coming from (source IPs, and so on).

Alternatively, you can deploy multiple ADFS farms within your organization. The limitation with multiple ADFS farms is that you can only assign a UPN to a single farm and you cannot span a single UPN across multiple farms. To leverage multiple farms, you would need to be able to direct specific UPNs to each farm. As an example, you may assign `%username%@region1.com` to ADFS farm 1 in region 1, while `%username%@region2.com` would be assigned to ADFS farm 2 in region 2. To fulfill a base global infrastructure to support local regional logons, you may consider the following items:

- Region 1
    - ADFS Internal
        - Single primary internal server
        - Redundant internal server
        - Managed by software or hardware load balancing
    - ADFS Proxy
        - Redundant proxy servers

- ° Managed by software or hardware load balancing
- ° Directory Synchronization server

- Region 2
  - ° ADFS Internal
    - ° Single primary internal server
    - ° Redundant internal server
    - ° Managed by software or hardware load balancing
  - ° ADFS Proxy
    - ° Redundant proxy servers
    - ° Managed by software or hardware load balancing

The following diagram shows an example of a base global infrastructure to support local regional logons:

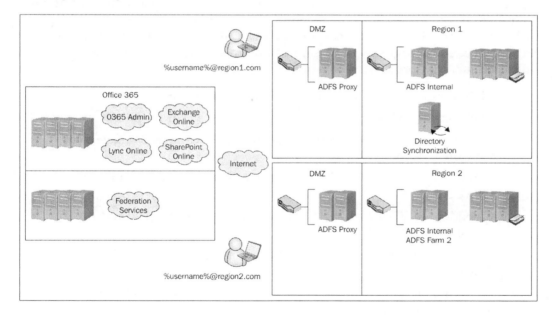

ADFS summary

At a fundamental level, a simple ADFS deployment does not require much complexity to offer your users a simplified logon to the service. The good news is that if you are planning to pilot the service, a basic infrastructure is all you need to get started. As you start to evaluate Office 365 further, you will start adding complexity to your core infrastructure, in order to support your business. In most cases, this is not significantly more complex than the services you have likely already planned and deployed for your users, meeting your existing general business requirements and SLAs.

Exchange Hybrid

Exchange Hybrid is really a rich coexistence option provided by Microsoft, by leveraging existing native Exchange tools. Exchange Hybrid offers customers with an existing Exchange 2003, 2007, or 2010 environment the capability to integrate directly your Office 365 subscription. Think of the integration as merely an extension of your environment. The integration components can be enabled, when a customer deploys Exchange 2010 (SP1+) in their environment. Integration is established by creating an Exchange Federation agreement from the on-premise Exchange Organization, to the Office 365 subscription. The benefits of Exchange Hybrid are:

- Mail routing through Exchange 2010, leveraging TLS
- Mail routing control (mail flow from/to Office 365 or on-premise)
- Simplified management from Exchange 2010, **Exchange Management Console (EMC)**
- Maintaining a long-term Exchange mailbox presence on-premise and in Office 365
- Calendar Free/Busy lookup between Exchange on-premise and Office 365 mailboxes
- Simplified mailbox moves between Exchange on-premise and Office 365 mailboxes
- Simplified desktop Outlook 2007+ conversion between Exchange on-premise and Office 365 mailboxes
- Single **Outlook Web App (OWA)** URL between Exchange on-premise and Office 365 mailboxes

As you plan for your deployment to Office 365, there are many areas you need to consider for your hybrid deployment. The following are the key areas that we will review:

- Is Exchange Hybrid the right fit?
- Exchange Hybrid deployment considerations
- Exchange Hybrid design examples
- Exchange Hybrid summary

Is Exchange Hybrid the right fit?

The answer to the question, "Is Exchange Hybrid the right fit?", is easier for organizations with a single Exchange Organization consisting of Exchange 2003, 2007, or 2010 in your existing AD environment. The answer to this question gets more complicated if you have a hosted Exchange environment or you are leveraging a non-Exchange messaging system. The reason for this is due to the requirements of an Exchange Hybrid deployment. Exchange Hybrid requires the following:

- Office 365 Directory Synchronization in the same AD environment as the Exchange Hybrid server
- The existing AD must be Windows Server 2003 forest functional mode or higher
- Mailbox moves by the Hybrid server have to occur from the existing Exchange organization, leveraging Office 365 Directory Synchronization

If you currently have an Exchange Organization and you can connect the Directory Synchronization server to the same AD environment for a long term, deploying an Exchange Hybrid server will be an advantage. Some of the key advantages are:

- By deploying an Exchange Hybrid server, you will greatly simplify the mailbox migration process to Office 365
- By simplifying this process, you are cutting down the need to introduce third-party tools for either migration or coexistence
- Enables the ability to perform a staged migration versus a flash cut over
- Greatly improved user experience during a migration by not causing users to re-download their cached mailbox, providing them with a rich coexistence experience

If you currently have a disconnected Exchange Organization (hosted or you are being split off from another company) or you have a non-Exchange messaging system, a Hybrid server may not provide you with a significant advantage. The reasons why you may want to deploy an Exchange Hybrid server, in this scenario, are as follows:

- You plan to maintain an on-premise messaging system and want it tightly connected to your Office 365 subscription
- You plan to use this infrastructure as a swing infrastructure to speed up migrations from an existing messaging system
- You have applications that depend on connecting directly to an Exchange Organization (not necessarily for open-relaying)

If you choose not to deploy an Exchange Hybrid server, or the Exchange Hybrid server does not fit your environment, you will be dependent on third-party tools to perform the migrations and if necessary to create coexistence with Office 365. Leveraging third-party tools does increase complexity and costs, but there are some great third-party tool options that can simplify this process. We will review those tools in the *Exchange Hybrid deployment considerations* section.

Exchange Hybrid deployment considerations

An Exchange Hybrid server can be deployed in almost any environment connected to Office 365 by Active Directory and the Office 365 Directory Synchronization server. When you plan to deploy an Exchange Hybrid server, you need to consider several items:

- Location of your existing messaging system and users
- Migration bandwidth for the Hybrid server
- Scaling your Hybrid server (including availability services)
- Exchange Schedule Free/Busy Store

Let's review these items and their importance.

Location of your existing messaging system

You may have a centralized or distributed messaging system. Likewise, you may have subscribed to the Office 365 service in one of the three major regions. If you maintain a centralized messaging system, it may be important to locate an Exchange Hybrid server at that location. By locating the Hybrid server closest to your existing centralized messaging system, you will prevent latency and possible corruption when migrations occur.

Also, if you have a centralized messaging system, you may have adequate bandwidth to support the query attempts made by end users when performing user information lookups such as free/busy, and so on.

If you have a distributed messaging system, you may have to consider the following:

- Are the users leveraging the same e-mail namespace across all systems?
- If users are leveraging a different e-mail namespace across regions, can you break down the namespace and regions, and group them together for a distributed Hybrid deployment?
- Is there a primary site that all users eventually traverse to, in which you could locate the Hybrid server?
- If you are distributed across multiple regions and are there a larger number of users within the region in which you can locate a Hybrid server?

There are many more questions that can be asked when planning your Exchange Hybrid server deployment. In most cases, the Hybrid server will follow existing Exchange 2010 architectural decisions. We will review the various design examples in the *Exchange Hybrid design examples* section.

Migration bandwidth for the Hybrid server

If you have an existing Exchange Organization, you are likely planning a migration while leveraging the Hybrid servers. Bandwidth is a critical component when you position this Hybrid server. If your organization has minimal bandwidth, both during business hours and off-business hours, you may need to consider renting additional bandwidth during the migrations. Otherwise, you may have to relocate the Hybrid server. If you have adequate bandwidth, the next step will be planning and testing your migration throughput. We will dive in deeper on migration throughput planning in *Chapter 7, Preparing for a Hybrid Deployment and Migration*.

Scaling your Hybrid server

Much like the location of your messaging system, the scale out of your Hybrid environment may be necessary. The key considerations for scaling your Hybrid environment are as follows:

- You plan to maintain a long-term Hybrid environment
- You plan to leverage multiple Hybrid servers in multiple environments
- You want to increase migration throughput for the various e-mail name spaces

While scaling out your Hybrid servers may be an advantage, it's important to plan how your users will leverage these servers or if they will be used at all. Currently, the Hybrid servers respond to users' requests based on the services provided. As an example, if you have Autodiscover set up, it's likely that only a load balancer or array will respond to that lookup for the namespace specified.

Exchange schedule Free/Busy store

Office 365 does not support the use of Public or System folders. When a user is migrated to Office 365, they start to leverage the availability service for Free/Busy lookups, the **Offline Address Book (OAB)**, and other services such as the Out-of-Office Assistant.

If you have Public folders in place today, it's important to note that any users migrated to Office 365 will not be able to leverage Public folders, once moved in to Office 365.

On the other hand, you may have the Free/Busy store within your environment. Office 2003 and earlier leveraged Exchange Free/Busy information within the system store. When building a Hybrid deployment, you will need to provide Free/Busy information to Exchange 2003/Office 2003 users, while leveraging the Exchange Hybrid server. This means, the Exchange Hybrid store maintains a System folder for the Office 365 users, while in coexistence. The positioning of this server(s) and the System folder replicas will be important to all users leveraging this store for lookups.

The distribution of this system store will be important for Exchange 2003/Office 2003 users, as delays may cause inaccessibility to Office 365 user's Free/Busy information.

Exchange Hybrid design examples

An Exchange messaging organization can be deployed in many ways. Likewise, an Exchange Hybrid deployment can follow a similar approach. Optimizing the positioning of your Exchange Hybrid deployment is critical in both migrations and client response times. Some examples of a complete deployment, including ADFS integration are as follows:

- Centralized Exchange organization
- Distributed Exchange organization
- Disconnected Exchange organization or non-Exchange messaging environment

Centralized Exchange organization

The following diagram shows an example of a centralized Exchange Organization with the Exchange Hybrid server deployed in the same site. The Exchange Hybrid server maintains the Federation agreement with Office 365 and all mail routing to/from Office 365:

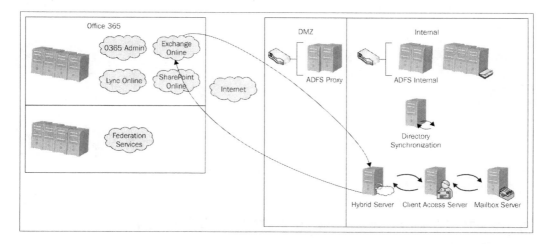

Distributed Exchange organization

The following diagram shows an example of a distributed Exchange organization with the Exchange Hybrid server deployed in multiple sites. The Exchange Hybrid server maintains the Federation agreement with Office 365 and all mail routing to/from Office 365. However, in this example, the additional Exchange Hybrid server manages Autodiscover/availability services for the other sites. If the first Hybrid server becomes unavailable, the Federation Trust needs to be transferred:

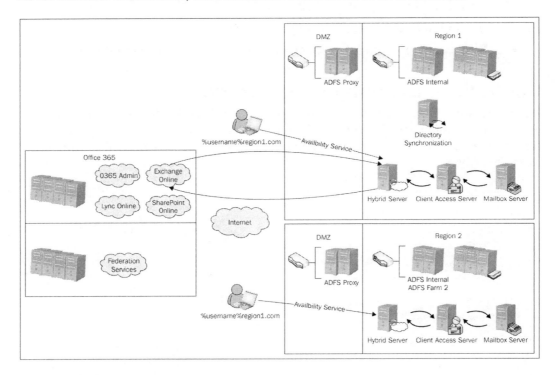

Disconnected Exchange organization or non-Exchange messaging environment

In this scenario, the Exchange Hybrid server's purpose would only be to manage mailboxes you plan to keep on-premise long-term or you plan to use the Exchange Hybrid server as a swing server to Office 365. In this case, it's unlikely you already have an Exchange organization deployed. The following are examples of these two approaches:

- Maintaining on-premise Exchange mailboxes for a long term:

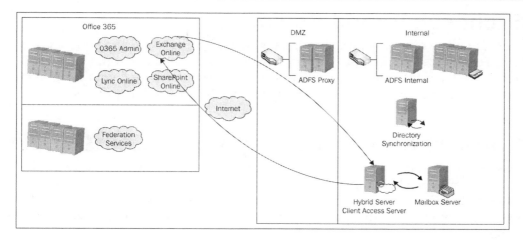

- Using Exchange Hybrid as a swing migration environment:

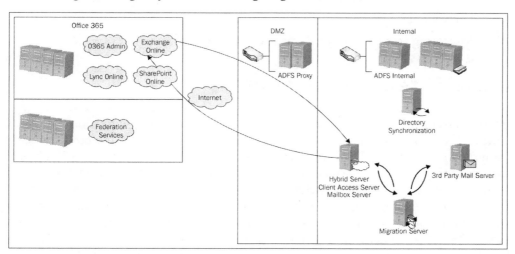

Although an Exchange Hybrid server is not required to perform migrations to Office 365, in this example a Hybrid server is used for a number of reasons that include:

- Plans to keep some mailboxes on premise for a long term
- Increase the performance of a migration to Exchange for the end users, minimizing third-party coexistence requirements
- Third-party coexistence tools do not exist for your messaging system
- Storage is not a limitation
- Bandwidth is a limitation, therefore making a staged migration from Exchange Hybrid a more attractive solution

Exchange Hybrid Summary

There are many options when planning for an Exchange Hybrid server. Whether you have a centralized environment, distributed or disconnected environment, there is an architecture that fits your organization. Once you have completed your integration planning for Office 365, you will be ready to start the preparation process.

Non-Exchange messaging systems

Believe it or not, not everyone has a Microsoft Exchange messaging system within their environment. Although we are not focused on non-Exchange messaging systems, it's still an important topic when working towards an understanding of how to integrate with Office 365. The key items of focus for non-Exchange Messaging Systems are:

- Active Directory readiness
- Coexistence options
- Migrating from a Non-Exchange messaging system

Active Directory readiness

If you are managing a non-Exchange system, you already know that your Active Directory environment may not match your existing messaging environment. As an example, if you have Lotus Notes or GroupWise environments, these environments do not depend on Active Directory for authentication. Because of this, it's likely that your messaging users may not be an exact match to your Active Directory users. In fact, even if they match, the attributes may not look the same. When you plan to migrate a non-Exchange messaging system, it's necessary that you update Active Directory if you plan to leverage Office 365 Directory Synchronization. When you leverage Directory Synchronization, you create your Office 365 Address Book, for all of the services you leverage. This address book is critical, as it provides the following:

- Entries in the Exchange **Global Address List (GAL)**, providing your migrated users the ability to e-mail users who are still on-premise
- SharePoint Security Groups and a general user list
- Lync Address Book, enabling you to add people within your organization to your contact list

By having inaccurate data within the address book, you risk users not finding who they are trying to address and this will result in Non Delivery (NDR) e-mail messages due to an invalid or inaccurate e-mail address information in Active Directory.

Having accurate data within Active Directory will enable you to smooth out both your coexistence and migration options. If you leave inaccurate data in Active Directory, after you start this process, you are likely going to cause some pain to your users.

Coexistence options

There are two types of coexistence options, when considering a migration from one platform to another; these are:

- Basic coexistence
- Rich coexistence

Basic coexistence

Basic coexistence is the ability to provide a unified address book and efficient mail routing between the mail systems. Out of the box, if you leverage Office 365 Directory Synchronization, you should be able to achieve this.

Rich coexistence

In addition to basic coexistence, rich coexistence also provides the users the ability to communicate with little differentiation between mail systems (includes translation of calendar invites, rich text in e-mails, and so on). Rich coexistence should also enable the ability to see calendaring information between the two systems (for example, free/busy).

There are many tools to provide this type of coexistence. Some require a coexistence server to be deployed, which manages all the traffic to/from Office 365 and the on-premise mail system. Other tools provide synchronization of mailboxes between the systems.

Migrating from a Non-Exchange messaging system

The Exchange Hybrid server offers a great way to migrate users from on-premise Exchange environments to Office 365. So what do you do when you don't have an on-premise Exchange environment or have a hosted Exchange environment? You leverage one of the following methods:

- Use the simple migration method provided by Office 365 (ideal for smaller organizations)
- Purchase a third-party tool specialized in migrating from your source messaging environment to Office 365

Migrating any mail is certainly not the easiest option; purchasing a third-party tool is likely to be the most ideal option. Third-party tools typically offer the following benefits:

- Translating of e-mail addresses from the source messaging system to Office 365 (for example, converting a Lotus Notes e-mail address to an SMTP address)
- Enabling the ability to scale up a number of migration consoles to increase the performance of the migration and number of mailboxes/data you can migrate
- Providing reporting, enabling you to proactively repair or notify users of a problematic migration of their mailbox

Certainly migrations from unlike messaging systems are not perfect, but leveraging third-party tools will help streamline and smooth out the process by addressing some complexities with manually moving users and easing the desktop e-mail transition. In most cases, it's recommended to bring in experts that know how to leverage those tools, if you move forward with them.

Summary

Office 365 provides a nice set of basic and rich integration options for both Exchange and non-Exchange messaging systems. We learned about the base integration options to enable a simplified logon process for users to an extended integration option, enabling rich coexistence for on-premise and Exchange Online organizations. These options should help you work through your planning process, preparing you for the deployment of these options.

Based on the integration options for professionals, small businesses, and enterprises, you have to decide which path is correct for your organization. If you choose to leverage the professional or small business path, then the next chapter is a right fit for you, If you plan to leverage the enterprise path, you may want to skip ahead to *Chapter 7, Preparing for a Hybrid Deployment and Migration*.

5
Preparing for a Simple Migration

So far in this book, we have prepared you for purchasing and beginning to use Office 365. However, a key factor yet to be completed is migrating mailbox content from your existing mail system.

In this chapter, we will discuss the various options available for performing a migration to Exchange Online and what needs to be done to prepare your environment for migration. We'll cover the following topics:

- Overview of a simple migration
- Available migration options
- Differences between source platforms
- The migration process
- Getting ready

A simple migration

When an organization looks to migrate mail in a single direction to Exchange Online, it is called a **simple migration** due to the fact that it is one way.

Organizations looking to retain on-premise Exchange Server functionality, as well as utilize Exchange Online would choose a hybrid environment over a simple migration. A hybrid environment is a mixture of both environments which is more complex to implement and maintain than a simple migration. We discuss these further in *Chapter 7, Preparing for a Hybrid Deployment and Migration* and *Chapter 8, Deploying a Hybrid Infrastructure: ADFS.*

Migration options

There are really only five main mail platform types used by the organizations that wish to migrate to Exchange Online. These are as follows:

- POP e-mail systems
- IMAP e-mail systems
- Hosted Exchange Server
- Gmail or Google Apps
- Exchange Server 2003 or 2007

Based on these platforms, we have created several scenarios which are reflective of common customer environments and situations.

POP e-mail

Many small businesses currently utilize POP e-mail provided by their domain name or website host. These are the simplest of migrations as the mailbox content is migrated by relying on the PST file import functionality in Outlook. Users simply need to import their existing PST file into the new Exchange Online mailbox.

IMAP

Some organizations may be utilizing IMAP either from a hosted service provider or an on-premise server (such as Novell GroupWise). These mail systems can be imported natively by using the migration wizard within the Exchange Online control panel. It is important to note that IMAP only contains mail objects and folders (not calendars, contacts, tasks, or any other Outlook-based items as these are stored in PST files).

Hosted Exchange or Gmail

For organizations that have already made a move to cloud services and are using e-mail from either a hosted Exchange Server provider or Gmail (or Google Apps) they are better off utilizing third-party, cloud-based migration systems. An example of this would be www.migrationwiz.com which allows the mailbox content to be moved from the original mailbox directly into the new Exchange Online mailbox.

Exchange Server 2003 or 2007

It is quite common to find organizations still running Exchange Server 2003 or 2007 either as a standalone solution or as part of the Small Business Server 2003 or 2008.

Effectively, all that is required is the enabling of RPC over HTTP for any of the versions. However, this can prove to be challenging as the functionality was not native to Exchange Server/SBS 2003.

In Exchange Server 2007/SBS 2008, however, there are more complexities around the provisioning of the actual certificates and utilization of the Autodiscover functionality.

The actual migration is performed by running the migration wizard within the Exchange Online control panel.

Staged migration

A staged migration allows you to choose which mailboxes get migrated to Exchange Online and move at your own pace. During this process, however, users of both Exchange Server on-premise and Exchange Online are in separate environments. As a result, these users will not have access to a shared Global Address List or Free/Busy information.

During the migration all e-mails that are routed via the on-premise Exchange Server are also retained locally, which provides for rollback if required.

Cutover migration

A cutover migration will simply begin the process of migrating all mailboxes from your on-premise Exchange Server to Exchange Online in a single step.

Migration option comparison

For simple digestion of the scenarios discussed earlier, we have broken down the difference between options into the following table and listed requirements for each:

Migration type/ Requirements	PST migration	IMAP	Third-party tool	Exchange staged	Exchange cutover
Server access	No	No	Possibly	Yes	Yes
Directory Synchronization	No	No	No	Yes	No
Define your own migration schedule	Yes	Yes	Yes	Yes	No

Migration type / Requirements	PST migration	IMAP	Third-party tool	Exchange staged	Exchange cutover
SSL certificate purchase	No	No	Possibly	Yes	Yes
PC access to migrate content	Yes	Yes	No	No	No

The migration process—in a nutshell

The steps involved in the actual migration process will differ, depending on the option chosen.

Effectively they will follow the same basic pattern:

1. Creating users' accounts
2. Activating Exchange Online mailboxes
3. Migrating mailbox content

Generally the **Mail eXchange** (**MX**) record is cut over after the completion of a successful mailbox migration however some administrators prefer to do this beforehand to ensure that no new mail items are left behind.

However, the key to a successful migration is not the actual mailbox content migration itself, it is the planning and preparation.

Planning for migration

Several key factors must be addressed when planning the migration to Exchange Online to ensure it is done successfully.

These are both technical factors, as well as human factors.

Technical considerations

There are numerous technical considerations which must be taken into account when planning for a migration. Some of the more common questions are as follows:

- Which of the above example scenarios mirrors yours?
- Have users been informed of the change?
- How much data can you send through your Internet link to Exchange Online (meaning how many gigabytes of mail can be uploaded)?

- Does your monthly Internet download allowance cater for the mailboxes being downloaded back into the Outlook .OST file for each user?

- Do you plan to start users on Exchange Online with their full mailbox or just a portion of the recent content?

- Do you have access to all desktops so you can configure the new account in Outlook?

- How many computers will you have to re-configure, and do you have the resources to do them all in the timeframe?

Asking such questions will help determine your migration plan.

For example, if you have 80 users each with mailboxes of 5 GB then it is not likely that you will be able to transfer 400 GB of data in a single weekend. This is especially important as Exchange Online only supports mailbox transfer speeds of 500 MB per hour (higher speeds can be achieved by raising a support ticket before commencing the migration). Therefore, you would most likely go for a staged migration approach (if using Exchange Server) or alternatively a third-party solution such as www.migrationwiz.com which allows multiple mailbox copy passes.

People considerations

Another key element of any migration plan is change management and a communication plan with a view to ensure that the end user experience is not a negative one.

It is important to notify users of any changes to their day-to-day operations that may impact on their productivity as any disruption could further delay the migration or leave a sour taste in their mouth.

A part of the change management is to inform users about the migration procedure at a high level so that they are made to feel a part of the process.

There will also be an element of re-configuring desktops and mobile devices. So the more comprehensive your change management and communications, the more you will be able to empower the users to do the work themselves.

Preparing your environment for migration

Before beginning the migration process, it is important to ensure that your environment has been prepared and that all requirements have been met.

Due to the varying requirements and processes we have broken these down between types of migrations.

PST-based migrations are not documented as they are merely a file import procedure which requires no preparation.

IMAP

In order for Exchange Online to access your IMAP sever/service, it must be accessible via the IMAP protocol from the Internet, which is generally the case.

It is important that the users be created via the Office 365 administrative interface either individually or in bulk.

You also need to prepare a listing of existing IMAP mailboxes in CSV format which is imported into the Exchange Online control panel. This CSV maps the IMAP credentials (e-mail address, username, and password) to the Exchange Online mailbox.

Hosted Exchange/Gmail

When migrating to Exchange Online from a hosted Exchange or Gmail environment you will generally have less access to the environment and as such, less preparation work can be done.

The process will be similar to that of IMAP whereby users are created in Office 365, followed by you working through the process of the third-party provider to get access to the existing mail system and have the migration provider (for example, MigrationWiz) move the content directly.

Exchange 2003 and Exchange 2007

A requirement of preparing to migrate to Exchange Online from Exchange Server 2003 and 2007 is to ensure that the server can be reached using the RPC over HTTPS (Outlook Anywhere) method on port 443.

 You must have a valid SSL certificate installed from a trusted root Certificate Authority. Self-signed SSL certificates issued by your server will not work as they are not recognized as "trusted" by external sources.

To ensure that your Exchange Server is accessible by Office 365 and ready for migration it is recommended that you test Outlook Anywhere by using the Microsoft Remote Connectivity Analyzer (`www.testexchangeconnectivity.com`). To do this, follow these steps:

1. Select the **Outlook Anywhere** test to be run, as shown in the following screenshot:

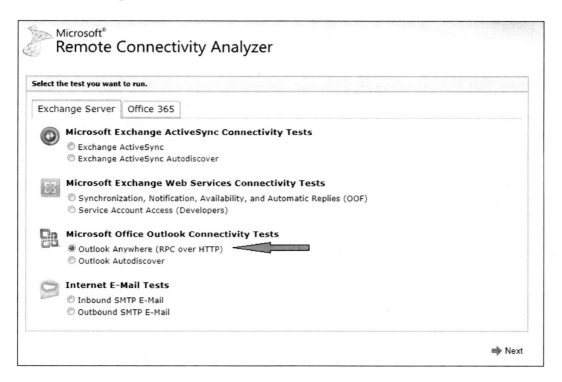

2. If you are using Exchange Server 2007 and already have Autodiscover working then select the **Use Autodiscover to detect settings option**:

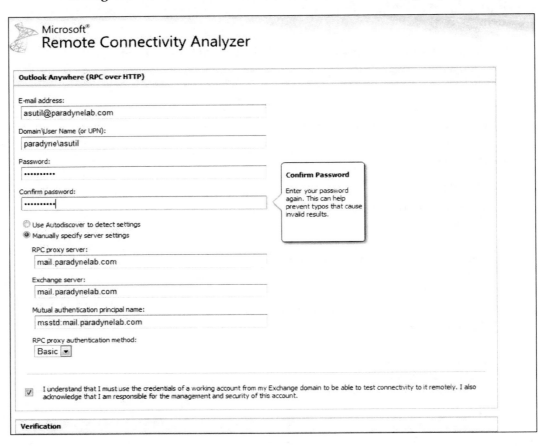

Alternatively, if you do not have Autodiscover, or are using Exchange Server 2003, you will need to input various pieces of information to enable the Analyzer to connect to, and interrogate, your server.

3. If your environment is correctly configured the tests will complete successfully (with or without warnings):

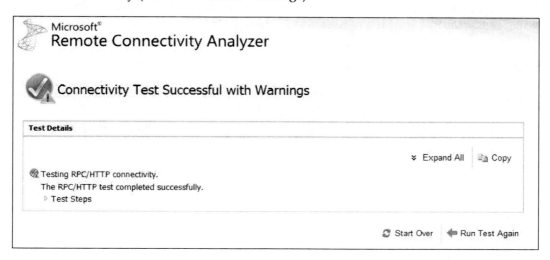

If the test fails, you will need to work through the issues listed to remediate them before attempting to run the Analyzer again.

It is imperative that you achieve a successful test before attempting to perform a migration to Exchange Online.

Requirements for a staged versus cutover migration

If you plan to perform a cutover migration of your Exchange Server to Exchange Online, there is no additional requirement for the implementation of the Microsoft Online **Directory Synchronization (DirSync)**.

Conversely, however, a staged migration cannot be performed without the prior implementation of DirSync.

It is important to note that DirSync cannot be installed on a domain controller, which can potentially be an issue in a single-server environment such as that of the Small Business Server 2003 or 2008. If you are in this situation then you will either need to join another server to your Active Directory domain purely for the purpose of installing DirSync, or choose to perform a cutover migration instead.

Summary

In this chapter, we have walked you through some of the common scenarios seen when performing a simple migration to Exchange Online.

By now, your environment should be ready and both you and your users should be ready to make the final step and begin migrating your e-mails to the cloud.

In the next chapter, we'll cover the steps required to perform the actual migration so that you can leave your existing mail platform in the dust!

6

Performing a
Simple Migration

So far throughout this book we have guided you in getting your Office 365 environment up and running, as well as the options available for your organization.

In the previous chapter we walked you through the steps for preparing your environment for a simple migration to Exchange Online, as well as provided you with an overview of migration options.

In this chapter we will walk you through those various options to get you migrated to Exchange Online successfully. We'll cover:

- Migrating from non-Exchange Server systems
- Migrating from Exchange Server

Migration from non-Exchange Server systems

If you are currently using an e-mail system that is not based on Exchange Server 2003 or 2007, the migration is not as seamless as moving directly from Exchange. However, it is still almost as quick and easy.

The two main steps involved in performing a simple migration from a non-Exchange system involve creating the user accounts in Office 365, and then performing a mailbox content migration using one of several methods.

Creating user accounts

If you are creating more than a handful of users it is recommended that you create the accounts using the bulk account creation method, as this will save a considerable amount of time.

This involves populating a **Comma-separated Values** (CSV) file with information about your users and uploading it into the Office 365 admin console.

While the CSV file allows you to populate many fields with user information, the two key fields required in order to create any user account are described in the following table:

Field	Description
User Name	The maximum total length of the username is 79 characters (including the @ symbol). It must be in the `name@ domain.<extension>` format. The user's alias cannot exceed 30 characters and the domain name cannot exceed 48 characters.
Display Name	The display name can be up to 256 characters long. Usually it's the full name of the person

It is also recommended that you fill out the **First Name** and **Last Name** fields—each of which is limited to 64 characters.

CSV files must follow the same format every time so if you choose to leave any fields blank, you must use a comma before moving on to the next field.

An example of using **User Name**, **First Name**, **Last Name**, and **Display Name** fields looks like:

```
Tony@paradynelab.com,Tony,Sarno,Tony Sarno,,,,,,,,,,,
```

If we choose to use just the required fields—**User Name** and **Display Name**—the result would look like:

```
Tony@paradynelab.com,,,Tony Sarno,,,,,,,,,,
```

Despite the fact that we have not used the **First Name** or **Last Name** fields, we had to still put a comma to allow the CSV reader in Office 365 to treat the field as blank. The additional commas shown after the full name in the preceding example refer to other fields; for example, **Department**, **Phone number**, **Country**, and many others that are commonly left blank.

You do not need to necessarily generate a CSV file yourself as a sample CSV file can be obtained from the **Users** section of the Office 365 administration portal. To obtain this sample CSV file or to begin importing your created CSV file, go to **New** | **Bulk add**, as shown in the following screenshot:

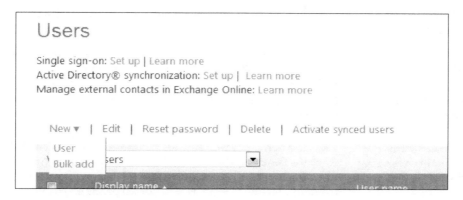

You can select to download a blank CSV file that you can start using straight away, or download a sample to see an example of how to fill it out with all the fields used:

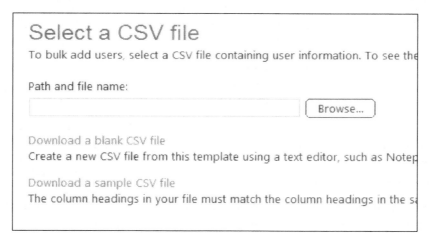

Once the users have been created you will be presented with a list of the created accounts and their temporary passwords. This list can also be sent to your current e-mail address for reference purposes. This list can also be used to provide each user with their initial login credentials.

Importing mailbox content

At this point you will need to determine which approach you should take for importing mailbox content.

The following table will provide you with some guidance on selecting the best option:

Current mail setup	Recommended migration method	Requirements
A few users with POP3 mailboxes using Outlook	Import PST files to new mailboxes	Outlook
Many users with POP3 mailboxes using Outlook	Use the Microsoft PST Capture Tool. Alternatively, third-party tools, available from organizations such as www.messageops.com may be used.	Outlook (x64) that can be downloaded from http://www.microsoft.com/download/en/details.aspx?displaylang=en&id=28767
IMAP-based mail system	Exchange Online built-in migration tool. Many Office 365 customers and partners prefer www.migrationwiz.com to perform migrations from hosted mailbox systems to Exchange Online.	CSV files
Google Apps	MigrationWiz	CSV files
		Access to all mailboxes
Other hosted mail systems	MigrationWiz	CSV files
		Access to all mailboxes

As third-party mail solutions are not supported by Microsoft, it is recommended that you engage the supplier directly or a Microsoft Office 365 partner.

IMAP migration

To begin a migration from IMAP systems using the built-in Exchange Online system, log in to the Exchange Online control panel in Office 365. Click on the **E-mail Migration** tab, click on **New**, and select **IMAP**, as shown in the following screenshot:

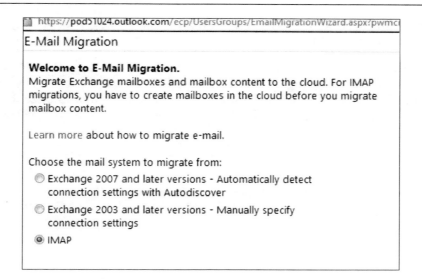

You will then need to enter your IMAP server details to begin the process. The IMAP server name is the fully qualified domain name (FQDN) used on the Internet to access the server. You should have information for this and the other fields configured in your current mail program, or this information is provided by your mail provider:

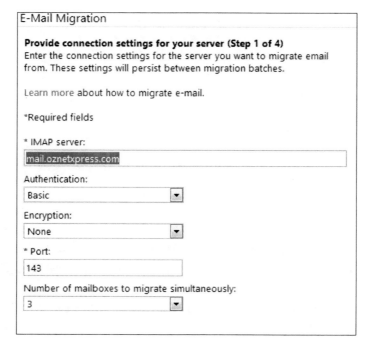

The wizard will check connectivity to your IMAP server using your settings before proceeding to the next screen.

On successful connection to your IMAP server you will have the option to exclude certain folders from being migrated to Exchange Online. Unless absolutely required it is recommended to exclude Trash folders or Deleted Items to minimize the mailbox content and time required to migrate. At the time of writing, only up to 50,000 items can be migrated (including Calendar and Contacts):

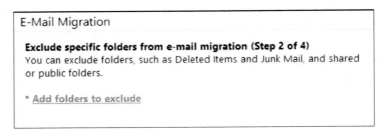

At this point you will need to create a separate CSV file with access to all mailboxes on your system, that will allow Exchange Online to connect to the mailboxes and retrieve the content:

The CSV file you create should be in the following format:

```
EmailAddress,UserName,Password
```

These fields are explained as follows:

- `EmailAddress`: It specifies the user ID for the user's cloud-based mailbox.
- `UserName`: It specifies the user logon name for the user's mailbox on the IMAP server.
- `Password`: It is the password for the user's account in the IMAP messaging system.

The CSV file contents would look like the following:

```
firstname.lastname@domain.com,firstname.lastname,password
```

Once the file is uploaded, click **Next** to validate the user mailboxes and proceed to the last step:

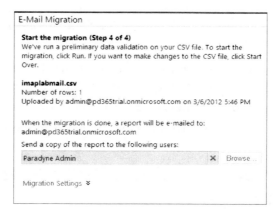

It is highly recommended that you specify a mailbox for sending the migration report to the users.

After clicking on **Run**, the dialogue box will disappear and you will be able to monitor the status of your migration from the Migration panel in the Exchange Online control panel:

Migrating from Exchange Server

If you are migrating from an existing Exchange Server environment the steps are relatively similar. As the Office 365 Small Businesses and Professionals plan does not allow Directory Synchronization we have limited the scope of this section to a cutover migration method.

The key steps involved in performing a migration from an on-premise Exchange Server are:

1. Ensure that remote connectivity is possible using RPC over HTTP (as discussed in *Chapter 5, Preparing for a Simple Migration*).
2. Grant the migration user full access to the mailboxes or mailbox store.
3. Run the Migration wizard from the Exchange Online control panel.

Granting access to all mailboxes in Exchange Server

Assuming that you have successfully prepared your Exchange Server environment to allow RPC over HTTP and tested it using the Exchange Remote Connectivity Analyzer, we can now move towards the steps involved in migrating the mailboxes.

The first task required is to allow the migration administrator permissions to access all of the mailboxes in order to migrate the contents to Exchange Online.

Assigning permissions in Exchange Server 2003

The process for this is relatively straightforward. Follow these steps:

1. Start Active Directory Users and Computers.
2. On the **View** menu, ensure that the **Advanced Features** checkbox is checked.
3. Select all the users you want to migrate, right-click on the selection, and click on **Properties**.
4. In the **Exchange Advanced** tab, click **Mailbox Rights**.
5. Click **Add**, select the migration administration account you are using, and click **OK**.
6. Make sure that the user is selected in the **Name** box. In the **Permissions** list, click **Allow** next to **Full Access**, and click **OK**.

Assigning permissions in Exchange Server 2007

In Exchange Server 2007 it is simpler to provide **Receive As** access to the entire mailbox database using PowerShell.

The cmdlet to do this is relatively straightforward:

```
Add-ADPermission -Identity "<Mailbox Store>" -User "<Migration
Administration Account>" -ExtendedRights Receive-As
```

Performing the mailbox migration

After the migration administrator has been given appropriate permissions on all mailboxes or mailbox databases, you can begin the actual migration process.

Log in to the Exchange Online control panel in Office 365, click on the **E-mail Migration** tab, and click **New**, as shown in the following screenshot:

A pop-up window will open requesting for the Outlook Anywhere configuration details. Enter the Migration administrator credentials and the Exchange Server details as used in the previous chapter for the Exchange Remote Connectivity Analyzer:

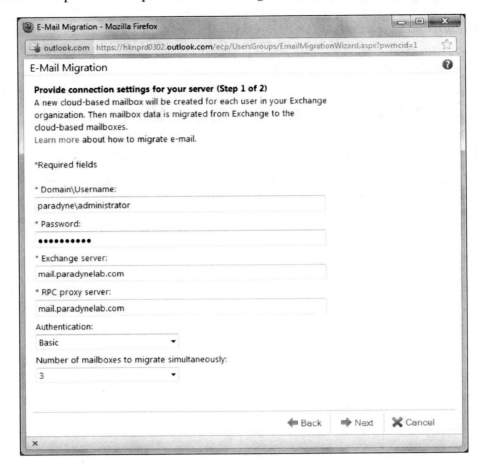

After entering all the details, click **Next**. The migration tool will test the connection to your Exchange Server again. After the connection is successful the following window will appear, where you can select the users who should be notified about the migration status:

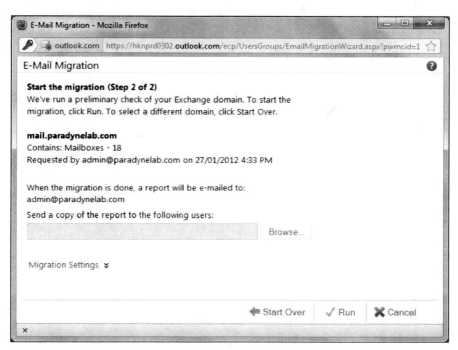

After you click **Run** the migration will begin immediately. The tool will populate the users in alphabetical order and create mailboxes for those users in Exchange Online (this is the default behavior and cannot be changed). The status of the migration can be seen in the Exchange Online control panel.

Summary

In this chapter we saw how to perform several potential methods available for performing migrations from a variety of systems to Exchange Online.

By now your migration should be well on its way and there are several post-migration considerations for you to review, which are covered in *Chapter 10, Deploying a Hybrid Infrastructure: Exchange Hybrid.*

7
Preparing for a Hybrid Deployment and Migration

By now you should have a relatively defined plan on what integration services you want to leverage from Microsoft Office 365, along with how you plan to scale out these services. Our next objective is to start preparing our environment for the integration services. In this chapter we will focus on working through the various core services available to Office 365 and their integration requirements for your environment. We will assume you have an existing Exchange Organization within your environment, consisting of Exchange 2010, or you are planning to add Exchange 2010 for this effort. We will focus on the following areas:

- Preparing your Office 365 subscription
- Active Directory preparation and readiness check
- Basic infrastructure preparation
- Defining the migration process

Preparing your Office 365 subscription

As you prepare for integration with Office 365, one of the first and most important steps is to ensure that you have registered all of your **User Principal Names (UPNs)**, and e-mail domains that you plan to use with the service. This also includes any e-mail domains you plan to coexist with, but leave on-premise. Let's recap on why both UPNs and e-mail domains are important to register.

In Active Directory, a UPN is an individual's logon name. In many cases, you are likely to use `domain\%username%` as the user's logon name. We need to change this to the user's UPN; for example, `%username%@domain` (in some cases it may be `domain.local` or a `public domain.com`.) We need to ensure that your UPN is a public domain. Ideally, we should have the public domain matching the user's primary e-mail address.

E-mail domains are also important for registering in Office 365. First off, you cannot assign a primary or secondary e-mail address to a mailbox, if the e-mail domain is not registered with the service. Also, if you choose to enable Exchange Hybrid, you will not be able to see the "free/busy" status for on-premise users if those e-mail domains (set as their primary e-mail address) are also not registered within the service. So it's important to register all e-mail domains you have assigned to users. If you do not plan to use that e-mail domain, or no longer need it, remove it from your users' `mail/proxyAddresses` attributes.

To register e-mail domains, you simply need to go to the Office 365 Admin portal at `https://portal.microsoftonline.com/Admin` and log on as a global administrator. Alternatively, you can also use the account with which you signed up to the service. Click on **Domains**:

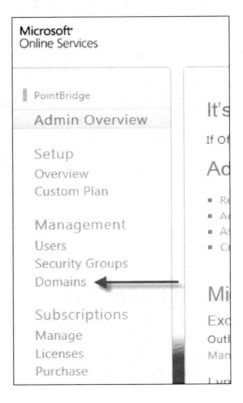

Now, add and verify all of the domains by repeating the following steps for each domain:

1. Click on **Add a domain**, as shown in the following screenshot:

2. Now, as shown in the following screenshot, enter the domain name you plan to add to your subscription:

3. You must now create a record within your DNS provider, to validate your domain. To do so, select either **General Information** or your DNS provider from the pull-down list. In this example, we will select **General Information**:

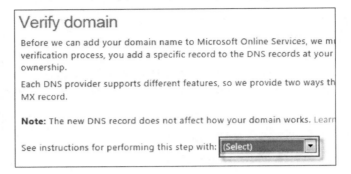

Arguably, the most optimal way to verify your DNS record is through a TXT record. Most DNS providers will allow you to create a TXT record within your service. If you do not see this option in your DNS admin console, contact your DNS provider to have one added manually. Microsoft will provide the TXT record information you need to add, as shown in the following screenshot:

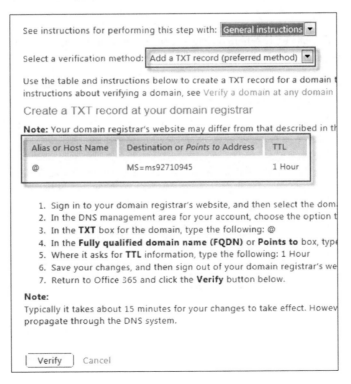

As an example, the following screenshot shows what the entry would look like, within your DNS service:

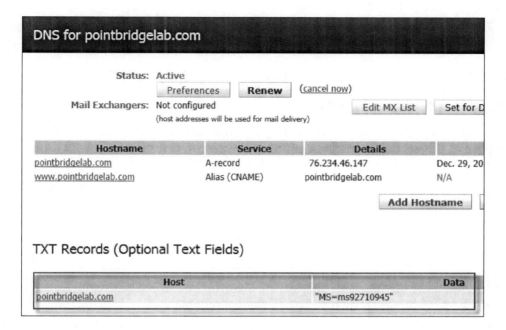

4. Once you have added your TXT record to your DNS provider, click on **Verify**. If your domain isn't verified successfully, you may need to wait until DNS propagates. You can come back and verify your domain at any time.

5. Once you click on **Verify**, select **Exchange Online** and click on **Next**. If the domain you added is the UPN that you also plan to use, you may want to select **Lync Online**, too:

6. Unless you plan to route all the mails directly to Office 365, skip the DNS settings section. (Also, do not make these DNS changes, if you plan to deploy an Exchange Hybrid server.)

7. Repeat these steps to add the remaining UPNs and e-mail domains.

Active Directory preparation and readiness check

Our next focus is to ensure **Active Directory (AD)** is ready for Office 365. The purpose of this section is to check your readiness to synchronize AD with Office 365, leverage ADFS, and enable Exchange Federation.

To easily identify the necessary changes, run the Microsoft Office 365 Readiness Tool (`http://community.office365.com/en-us/f/183/p/2285/8155.aspx#8155`). By running this tool, we will uncover the key changes that may be necessary to leverage the service. Once you run this tool, you will be able to identify the potential issues or changes required for:

- E-mail domains
- Forest/domain structure and Exchange schema
- Active Directory users, contacts, and group objects and single sign-on
- Desktop readiness

E-mail domains

As mentioned in the *Preparing your Office 365 subscription* section, be sure to add all your e-mail domains to the Office 365 Admin portal. This tool will highlight all e-mail domains discovered from users within your messaging system. If you are unaware of it, this tool will help you uncover those e-mail users. To easily find users with an e-mail domain attached to them, open **Active Directory Users and Computers** from a domain controller within your Exchange Organization. From there, do a custom search and select **Entire Directory**. As shown in the following screenshot, go to the **Advanced** tab and enter **proxyAddresses=smtp:*@<domain. com>** (**<domain.com>** being the domain you are searching for users that are bound to it):

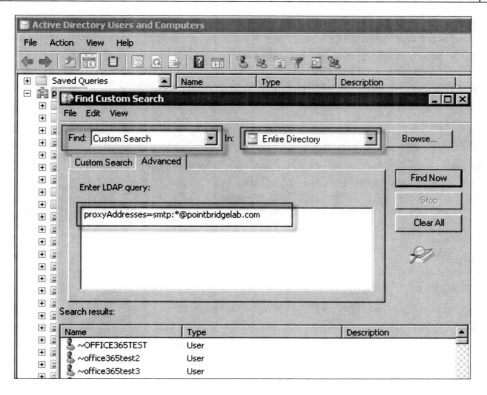

Forest/domain structure

Directory Synchronization and Active Directory Federation Services only support a single forest and all sub-domains under that forest. In addition to only supporting one forest, trust relationships cannot be used for authentication. All accounts must reside in the forest that you plan to synchronize. Verify that all the accounts you plan to synchronize will be accounts you plan to directly log on with. In addition, it's assumed that you have already deployed Exchange 2010 Service Pack 2.

Active Directory users, contacts, and group objects and single sign-on

Now review the Active Directory Cleanup and Office 365 Single Sign On and Identity sections for attribute updates that may be necessary.

The key items to address are mostly user, contacts, and group objects, when you integrate with Office 365. It's likely you will not have to change many of your user objects, unless you have steered far away from the AD best practices. The items that come up frequently are the unsupported characters applied to objects that will synchronize. The attributes you should review, as you prepare for synchronization, are covered in the following sections.

Users

Quite often, the following attributes cause conflict with directory synchronization, so review objects with these invalid characters:

- sAMAccountName: Invalid character examples are !, #, $, %, ^, &, {, }, \, /, `, ~, ", [,], :, @, <, >, +, =, ;, ?, and *

- displayName: Invalid character examples are ?, @, and +

- mail: Invalid character examples are [, !, #, $, %, &, *, +, \, /, =, ?, ^, `, {, }, and]

- mailNickname: Invalid character examples are ", \, /, [,], :, >, <, ;, and spaces

- proxyAddresses: Invalid character examples are [, !, #, $, %, &, *, +, \, /, =, ?, ^, `, {, }, and]

- userPrincipalName: Invalid character examples are }, {, #, ', *, +,), (, >, <, \, /, =, ?, and `

Groups

In order for a group to be mail-enabled, it requires a display name and an e-mail address. The same invalid characters for a user object, applies here.

Contacts

Contacts require a display name, proxy address and a target address. The same invalid characters for user objects apply here.

Desktop readiness

The reason why Office 365 has desktop requirements is primarily due to the Office 365 Service Sign-in Assistant. The Sign-in Assistant is supported by Windows 7, Vista SP2+, XP SP2+ and Mac OS X 10.5+. In this section, the readiness tool will identify operating systems that are not supported. You may have some computers that will show up in this report; however, those computers may also not exist.

As this report pulls from Active Directory, it is possible that you may have some old objects that have not been removed. Verify that your computers meet the minimum requirements for the Office 365 Service Sign-in Assistant, as well as the version of Office you plan to leverage.

Basic infrastructure preparation

To simplify our approach, let's start with a basic source Exchange 2010 environment. A diagram showing the scope of the requirements is as follows:

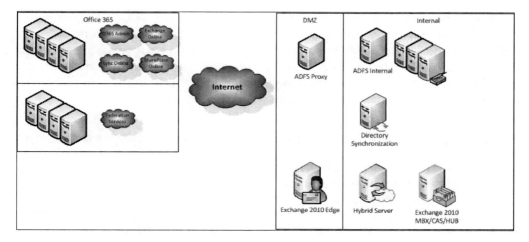

Let's focus on the necessary requirements for the following components:

- Directory Synchronization server
- Active Directory Federation Services
- Exchange Hybrid server

Directory Synchronization server

Only one Directory Synchronization server can be actively used within a single Office 365 subscription. The following are the base requirements for this server:

- 32-bit deployment—Windows Server 2003 SP2 or Windows Server 2008
- 64-bit deployment—Windows Server 2008 Standard or Windows Server 2008 R2
- AD domain joined within the forest that you plan to synchronize with Office 365

- Microsoft .NET Framework version 3.x installed
- Windows PowerShell 1.0 installed
- 1.6 GHz+ processor
- 4 GB RAM (16 GB for 50 to 100 K objects and 32 GB for 100 K+ objects)
- 100 MB or 1 GB NIC
- 100 GB+ free disk space for an object count less than 100 K (if you plan to synchronize over 50 K objects, you will need to consider deploying Directory Synchronization on a SQL server)

You need to provide the Directory Synchronization software with an Enterprise Admin account during installation. Beyond the installation, the Enterprise Admin privileges are no longer needed and are not saved. You will also need to provide an Office 365 Global Admin account. Create a dedicated account for the synchronization service. If you are required to change the password for this account, you will have to re-run the setup, to set those new credentials on this server.

Active Directory Federation Services (ADFS)

As we discussed in *Chapter 4, Integration Options for Enterprises*, you have many deployment scenarios which you can pursue for your ADFS farm(s). To keep things simple, we are going to focus on deploying a single ADFS internal and proxy server. Unless you plan to deploy more than five servers in a single farm or you plan to span servers across slow WAN links, or you have more than 60,000 users leveraging ADFS, proceed with these steps. If any of the previous items apply, you may need to consider deploying ADFS on a SQL environment. If you are a candidate for a larger farm or a more complex deployment, you can still follow these requirements, but you need to consider adding a SQL deployment to the mix.

To get started, let's cover the minimum server specifications, as we prepare for Office 365. These servers can be physical or virtual machines.

The specifications for ADFS 2.0 are as follows:

- Windows Server 2008 R2 (32-bit or 64-bit OS)
- AD domain joined (member only)
- 4 GB Ram
- Quad core 2 GHz
- 100 MB free disk space
- Microsoft .NET Framework version 3.5; SP1 installed
- Windows PowerShell 2.0 installed (with Windows Server 2008 R2 and .NET 3.51 to run the PowerShell cmdlets)

The requirements for the ADFS proxy server are as follows:

- Windows Server 2008 R2 (32-bit or 64-bit OS)
- Non-domain joined — recommended
- 4 GB RAM
- Quad core 2 GHz
- 100 MB free disk space
- Microsoft .NET Framework version 3.5; SP1 installed
- Windows PowerShell 2.0 installed (with Windows Server 2008 R2 and .NET 3.51 to run the PowerShell cmdlets)

One major key item to note about deploying both ADFS servers is their operating systems. Microsoft has packaged a different install for Windows Server 2008 versus 2008 R2. It is highly recommended that you keep both the internal and proxy servers at the same base operating system level. In addition, consider deploying both operating systems at either 32- or 64-bit (recommending 64-bit, to stay current).

Next, we will need to create service accounts, to manage all ADFS services. The following table shows some example service accounts:

Service account	Service account purpose
ADFS-Admin	The domain user account used for the ADFS Logon Service for the internal ADFS server farm.
	The domain user account with User access to the ADFS.
	Databases located on the SQL server will need SYS admin privileges on the SQL server temporarily during installation.
ADFS-Service	The local computer account used for the ADFS Logon Service for the ADFS proxy servers.
ADFS-Auth	Used for authentication between the ADFS server farm and the ADFS proxy server

Now let's prepare for the DNS entries that will be required for ADFS. For every domain create an internal and external DNS record. Your internal DNS record will point to your internal ADFS server, while your external DNS record will point to your ADFS proxy server. If you are using a load balancer or plan to deploy multiple ADFS servers, point these records to the virtual IP address of this load balancer.

The following table shows an example of the records you may create:

Type	Host	Points to Address	Where
A	sts.DOMAIN.com	ADFS VIP address	Internal DNS
A	sts.DOMAIN.com	ADFS Proxy VIP address	External DNS

Let's review the firewall rules you will need to enable:

- Create a firewall rule internal to your network to NAT, the virtual IP of the ADFS proxy server
- TCP 443 to and from the Internet to proxy server
- TCP 443 to and from the ADFS proxy server and the internal ADFS server farm

Finally, let's review what you should expect for certificate requirements.

- Third-party SSL certificates are required, to maintain a high level of security for Office 365 services (Subject Name = STS.Domain.com.)
- A Standard X.509 certificate will be used for securely signing all tokens that the federation server issues and that Office 365 will accept and validate.
- It is recommended to use the token-signing certificate generated by the ADFS server, as the ADFS server will auto-generate a new certificate prior to expiring.

The certificate guidelines are as follows:

- Ensure that the private key is exportable
- The Certificate's key length should be at least 2048 bits
- The signing algorithm should be either SHA-1 or SHA-256
- Valid for a long term (as this will be managing your authentication)
- Key usage must be both server authentication (1.3.6.1.5.5.7.3.1) and client authentication (EKU = 1.3.6.1.5.5.7.3.2)
- There should be no dotless subject names (for example, "servername" is not allowed)
- Must be from a well-known CA provider such as VeriSign, Entrust, and so on
- Root certificate authority is shared between the internal and proxy server
- SAN certificates can be used for the Exchange Hybrid implementation, but is not recommended for the ADFS implementation

Exchange Hybrid server

Our last integration component is an Exchange Hybrid server. Let's assume you have Exchange 2010 in your environment today. Let's assume we do not want to impact the existing Exchange 2010 server and we are going to add a single Exchange 2010 server to manage the Hybrid or integration with Office 365. To start out, let's identify some initial server requirements. The following are the base requirements for this server:

- Windows Server 2008 Standard or Enterprise and Service Pack 2 — 64-bit
- Windows Server 2008 R2 Standard or Enterprise — 64-bit
- .NET Framework 3.5 Service Pack 1
- IIS
- Windows PowerShell 2.0
- Windows Remote Management 2.0
- Exchange 2010 Service Pack 2 — 64-bit and latest Update Rollups (technically, Service Pack 1 is required, but for our upcoming examples, we will be using Service Pack 2. Service Pack 2 reduces the preparation down from 40+ steps in Service Pack 1 to only a few steps.)

The recommendations for the physical server are:

- x64-bit architecture/processor and 64-bit AMD
- 16 to 20 GB RAM
- Disk space
    - OS Partition 40 GB
    - Exchange installation and working directory 60 GB
- Quad core processor (minimum 2x processor cores)
- 1 GB NIC

The recommendations for the virtual server are:

- 64-bit Guest
- 16 to 20 GB RAM
- Disk space
    - OS Partition — 40 GB
    - Exchange installation and working directory — 60 GB
- 4 virtual processors
- 1 virtual NIC

In order to apply changes to the Exchange Organization, we need permissions to the Exchange Organization, as well as Global Administrator rights within Office 365.

We will need to create DNS records to help in routing mails to Office 365, as well as support the migration of the Outlook clients. The following tables show the recommended DNS additions that you may consider:

Domain verification

Type	Alias or hostname	Points to Address	TTL
CNAME	(MS record)	DOMAIN.com	1 Hour
CNAME	exchangedelegation. DOMAIN.com	Autodiscover.DOMAIN. com	1 Hour

Exchange Online

Type	Priority	Host	Points to Address	TTL
MX	0	service.DOMAIN.com	service-DOMAIN-com. mail.eo.outlook.com	1 Hour
CNAME	-	autodiscover.DOMAIN. com	autodiscover. outlook.com	1 Hour
CNAME	-	autodiscover.service. DOMAIN.com	autodiscover. outlook.com	1 Hour

Type	TXT Name	TXT Value	TTL
TXT	DOMAIN.com	v=spf1 include:outlook.com ~all	1 Hour
TXT	service.DOMAIN.com	v=spf1 include:outlook.com ~all	1 Hour
TXT	exchangedelegation. DOMAIN.com	xxxxxxxxxxxxxxxxxxxxxxxxxxxxxxx xxxxxxxxxxxxxxx	1 Hour
TXT	DOMAIN.com	xxxxxxxxxxxxxxxxxxxxxxxxxxxxxxx xxxxxxxxxxxxxxx	1 Hour

The above entries are used for the following:

- Service domain
    - Mail routing to Office 365, for migrated users
    - Auto-discover lookups

- Exchange delegation
  - ° Used to validate your domain, within the service
  - ° Also used for the Federation trust between on-premise and Office 365

Let's review the firewall rules you will need to enable:

- Create a firewall rule to the NAT (Exchange Hybrid) server IP. Allow port 25 to and from the internet to the Exchange Hybrid Server (An Exchange Edge 2010 server can also be used.)
- SMTP Relay (if required); TCP 587 and requires TLS.
- Mail routing (if required); TCP 25.

Often, organizations will ask what specific IPs the service connects to. Such questions come up, primarily, so that the firewall administrators can restrict traffic routing out of the organization. Microsoft provides a list, but recommends that you create exclusions by the names of the connecting service, rather than the IPs. To find the names and IPs for Exchange, go to `http://help.outlook.com/en-us/140/gg263350.aspx\`.

For Forefront Online, go to `http://technet.microsoft.com/en-us/library/hh510075.aspx`.

If you decide to track by IP, you may want to see the following RSS feed to ensure you are proactive in your changes:

`http://go.microsoft.com/fwlink/?linkid=236301`

Finally, let's review the certificate requirements for the Exchange Hybrid role. A public certificate is required, to set up Exchange Federation. A public certificate will essentially address both the Exchange Web Services and the Auto discover feature. In addition, the Exchange Federation trust can be self-signed with an internal CA or a public facing certificate. Exchange will automatically create a self-signed certificate, if one does not exist.

Defining the migration process

Now that we have started the process of provisioning your servers, we also need to start thinking about the migration process and the areas you need to also consider. At a high level, there a few areas we should prioritize. These areas include:

- Bandwidth evaluations (user connectivity and migration traffic)
- Using Public Folders
- Communicating and training

Bandwidth evaluations

While planning your migration to Office 365, bandwidth is an area that cannot be overlooked. Most organizations planning to move to Office 365, likely host their messaging infrastructure internally. This means, you likely to have not prepared your primary egress points for the traffic you are going to send over it. Much of your traffic may be internal or traversing over separate WAN links. When you move your users to Office 365, those users will now leverage the egress points you have in place for internet traffic.

There are two areas in which you need to be preparing your bandwidth for. Those two areas are the bandwidth you will use while migrating to Office 365 and your day to day bandwidth.

Migration bandwidth

Let's review the migration bandwidth needed to migrate to Office 365. There are many considerations when planning for bandwidth. These include:

- The total size of the data to be migrated
- Average mailbox size
- Number of users to be migrated and the logical breakdown of these users (for example, business units, facilities, and so on)
- The number of Exchange Hybrid (Client Access Servers) you have
- The amount of existing bandwidth you have
- Go-live helpdesk support capacity

Let's first start with how to estimate what you currently can achieve and if you need to expand further. First, let's start with a baseline of example information. Let's say we have an organization with the following information:

- 200 MB average mailbox size
- 500 GB of mailbox data
- 2,300 users and 200 shared resources
- 45 Mbps Internet connection

We can start by calculating what's possible. To do this, let's grab a simple calculator found at `http://www.dslreports.com/calculator`. Let's start by putting in our total mailbox data and our line speed, and then calculating the time:

Bandwidth Calculator

Enter two values, push Calc on the missing third value!

Data Size		Time		Speed	
500 GB		95444 s		45 Mbps	
Calc		Calc		Calc	
536,870,912,000 B	bytes (default)	100,079,991,719.3 ns	nanoseconds	45,000,000 bps	bits per second (default)
524,288,000 KB	kilobytes	97,734,366.9 ms	milliseconds	45,000 Kbps	kilo bits per second
512,000 MB	megabytes	95,443.7 s	seconds (default)	45 Mbps	mega bits per second
500 GB	gigabytes	1,590.7 m	minutes	5,625,000 Bps	bytes per second
0.5 TB	terabyess	26.5 h	hours	5,493.2 KBps	kilobytes per second
4,294,967,296,000 b	bits	1.1 d	days	5.4 MBps	megabytes per second
4,194,304,000 Kb	kilobits	0.2 w	weeks	27.8 T1	T1s
4,096,000 Mb	megabits			4.3 e10	10Mbps ethernet
4,000 Gb	gigabits			0.4 e100	100Mbps ethernet
3.9 Tb	terabits				

As you can see in the preceding screenshot, it will take approximately 26.5 hours on a maxed out 45 Mbps Internet connection to migrate 500 GB data. Realistically, you are likely using some of that 45 Mbps connection. Not to mention there is always bandwidth overhead. To be safe, you need to evaluate what's truly available, during your migration. In addition, you should add a buffer, so you are not planning for a full 45 Mbps connection.

Let's say you had minimal applications leveraging that 45 Mbps connection. It may be more realistic to plan for 30-35 Mbps of bandwidth, when planning your migration. That would look more like this:

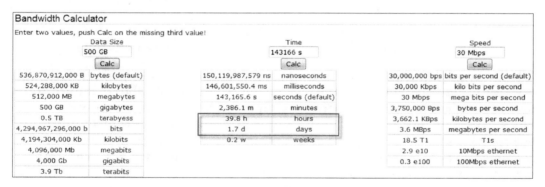

Bandwidth Calculator

Enter two values, push Calc on the missing third value!

Data Size		Time		Speed	
500 GB		143166 s		30 Mbps	
Calc		Calc		Calc	
536,870,912,000 B	bytes (default)	150,119,987,579 ns	nanoseconds	30,000,000 bps	bits per second (default)
524,288,000 KB	kilobytes	146,601,550.4 ms	milliseconds	30,000 Kbps	kilo bits per second
512,000 MB	megabytes	143,165.6 s	seconds (default)	30 Mbps	mega bits per second
500 GB	gigabytes	2,386.1 m	minutes	3,750,000 Bps	bytes per second
0.5 TB	terabyess	39.8 h	hours	3,662.1 KBps	kilobytes per second
4,294,967,296,000 b	bits	1.7 d	days	3.6 MBps	megabytes per second
4,194,304,000 Kb	kilobits	0.2 w	weeks	18.5 T1	T1s
4,096,000 Mb	megabits			2.9 e10	10Mbps ethernet
4,000 Gb	gigabits			0.3 e100	100Mbps ethernet
3.9 Tb	terabits				

Now, I know what you're probably thinking, "How can we spend 40 hours doing a migration?" Well, I probably would not. Most often, if you are planning to migrate as many users as possible, you are likely doing it over a weekend. When planning for a migration, I would consider only calculating bandwidth for half the weekend. (This gives you a nice buffer in the event you have migration issues.) Let's assume that the weekend is only 48 hours, which means you would only have 24 hours to migrate data.

Let's now focus on the data size in our calculations and set the time to 24 hours. That would look like this:

```
Bandwidth Calculator
Enter two values, push Calc on the missing third value!
           Data Size                        Time                           Speed
       324000000000                         24 h                          30 Mbps
          [ Calc ]                         [ Calc ]                       [ Calc ]
  324,000,000,000 B  bytes (default)    90,596,966,400 ns  nanoseconds    30,000,000 bps  bits per second (default)
      316,406,250 KB  kilobytes            88,473,600 ms  milliseconds        30,000 Kbps  kilo bits per second
      308,990.5 MB    megabytes               86,400 s   seconds (default)        30 Mbps  mega bits per second
        301.7 GB      gigabytes                1,440 m   minutes              3,750,000 Bps  bytes per second
          0.3 TB      terabyess                   24 h   hours                3,662.1 KBps  kilobytes per second
 2,592,000,000,000 b  bits                         1 d   days                    3.6 MBps  megabytes per second
 2,531,250,000 Kb     kilobits                   0.1 w   weeks                    18.5 T1  T1s
 2,471,923.8 Mb       megabits                                                    2.9 e10  10Mbps ethernet
     2,414 Gb         gigabits                                                    0.3 e100  100Mbps ethernet
       2.4 Tb         terabits
```

Based on calculations, it looks like the results are about 300 GB of data or 1,500 mailboxes, based on our average mailbox size. You now have some decisions to make. Those decisions may include the following:

- Do you plan to migrate in two or more weekends or a variety of non-business hour weeknights?

- Do you enforce cleanup on the source side, resulting in a smaller amount of data to be migrated?

- Can your helpdesk support the number of users you migrate, over a single weekend? (Calculate this based on iterations of pilot users testing.)

Whichever path you take, you will need to be able to support that path. As an example, do you have enough Exchange servers to support 30 Mbps of traffic? You may have to build two or more servers to support that. The best way to evaluate this is to build your first one or two CAS servers in an array. Test mailbox moves by creating a sampling of migrations in concurrency. Migrating one or two users at a time will now provide you with a sampling of what's realistic. Start with 50 mailboxes and evaluate the size of data migrated, along with the time it took to migrate a majority of those mailboxes when they are running concurrently. From there, you can determine if you have enough migration consoles or you need more.

User bandwidth

The amount of bandwidth a user needs is significantly different than the amount of bandwidth you need for a migration. **Migration bandwidth** is a point in time bandwidth, where user bandwidth is something that you will need to support day-to-day. To calculate this, we need to understand where and how your users work.

First, we need to divide your users up in to their egress points (collection of users going out of a specific Internet connection.) Let's say you have three sites, which look like the following:

- **Site 1**: 1,000 users; 100 Mbps Internet connection (40 percent utilized)
- **Site 2**: 700 users; 45 Mbps Internet connection (60 percent utilized)
- **Site 3**: 500 users; 10 Mbps Internet connection (50 percent utilized)

Now, let's figure out how these users use Outlook today. Refer to the following table provided by Microsoft, under the profile table in the Client Network Traffic section (`http://technet.microsoft.com/en-us/library/cc540453(EXCHG.80).aspx`) to categorize those users:

Activity	Light	Medium	Heavy	Very heavy
Messages sent per day	5	10	20	30
Messages received per day	20	40	80	120
Average message size	50 KB	50 KB	50 KB	50 KB
Messages read per day	20	40	80	120
Messages deleted per day	10	20	40	60
OWA log on and log off per day	2	2	2	2

Now let's determine what e-mail client they will be using (although Outlook 2007 is referenced, we can also apply this to Outlook 2010, as the stats are similar):

E-mail client	Light	Medium	Heavy	Very heavy
Office Outlook 2007	1,300 KB/day/ user	2,600 KB/day/ user	5,200 KB/day/ user	7,800 KB/day/ user
OWA	6,190 KB/day/ user	12,220 KB/day/ user	24,270 KB/ day/user	36,330 KB/day/ user

Let's say the Site 1 users fall in to the following categories:

E-mail client	Light	Medium	Heavy	Very heavy
Office Outlook 2007	100	500	200	100
OWA	50	40	10	

Now let's calculate what Site 1 would look like. To start, we need to know what the formulae are. Microsoft provides the following examples:

- If your company has 100 heavy Office Outlook 2007 users, here's how to calculate the average network traffic, measured in bytes per second:

  Network bytes/sec = (100 heavy users × (5,200 KB/user ÷ day)) ÷ (8 hr/day × 3600 sec/hr) = 18.5 KB/sec

  Assuming a daily peak of twice the average usage, your network connection would need to support approximately 37 KB/sec.

- If your company has 100 medium OWA users, here's how to calculate the average network traffic, measured in bytes per second:

  Network bytes/sec = (100 medium users × (12,220 KB/user ÷ day)) ÷ (8 hr/day × 3600 sec/hr) = 42.4 KB/sec

  Assuming a daily peak of twice the average usage, your network connection would need to support approximately 84.9 KB/sec.

Let's assume Site 1 users all work during the same business hours:

E-mail client	Bandwidth (KB/sec)				
	Light	Medium	Heavy	Very heavy	Total
Office Outlook 2007	10	91	73	55	229
OWA	22	34	17	0	73
Total	32	125	90	55	302

Based on these calculations, Site 1 would need 302 KB/sec of bandwidth or 2.5 Mbps during normal business hours. As Site 1 has a connection of 100 MB and only 40 percent is utilized, Site 1 should have enough bandwidth to support users connecting to Office 365.

Take this calculation example and apply it to all of the sites that have direct Internet bandwidth. To do so, consider the following:

- The total bandwidth available
- What the utilization is during normal business hours
- Calculate how your users will use the bandwidth, based on the above calculations
- Determine if there is enough available bandwidth, based on the calculated bandwidth required

If your Internet connection is also your WAN link to your data center, and you will continue to use the same Internet connection, you may be trading bandwidth for bandwidth. What I mean is, if you are removing Outlook/Exchange bandwidth over the same Internet connection, but adding at back for Exchange Online over the same WAN link… then you likely have a site you will not have to calculate. (Unless you are changing the Outlook connectivity method.)

Using Public Folders

Public Folders have been widely used by many organizations, back in the early Exchange days. These Public Folders have likely been migrated, during every Exchange upgrade, to your current one. Public Folders are not supported in Office 365 and will likely never be supported. This means you need to find an alternative use for Public Folders.

The challenge with Public Folders usually comes up when a large quantity are deployed and the regular cleanup has not occurred. If you do not have many Public Folders, your job is somewhat easy. If you have many, you may need to take a closer look at what's in use. In general, most organizations will convert Public Folders to Shared Mailboxes or SharePoint lists/libraries.

You can leverage third-party tools, such as the Public Folder Migrator for SharePoint (`http://www.quest.com/public-folder-migrator-for-sharepoint`). If you plan to migrate Public Folders to Shared Mailboxes, you can simply do this by adding a Shared Mailbox and opening it with Outlook 2010. From there, find your Public Folder and drag the contents from the Public Folder to the Shared Mailbox. You may have to perform other steps, such as assigning permissions or moving e-mail addresses to this new Shared Mailbox.

If you have a large quantity of Public Folders, you may need to evaluate what's in use today. To do this, you can grab a free Exchange tool called **PFDavAdmin**, found at:

```
http://www.microsoft.com/download/en/details.
aspx?displaylang=en&id=22427
```

With this tool, you can find out who owns a Public Folder, when it was last used, and so on. This should help you survey your Public Folder use and make an easy decision on what to archive off and what should be migrated.

Communications and training

Communications and training are two of the most important components of any migration plan of a major user service. When you plan to migrate users from one service to another, what they experience is how well communications were and what their go-live experience will be like.

Communicating with users on what to expect and what their experience will be like on day one is very important. Some of the communications you should consider are:

- The business announcement of the change, from someone on the leadership team such as a director or an executive
- The migration date for the user being migrated
- Migration expectations (examples)
  - How to log on to Outlook
  - How to communicate with non-migrated users
  - Reconfiguration of their mobile device
  - New service availability
  - Where to go for help! (FAQ site, different helpdesk numbers, who to find if helpers are walking the floors, and so on)
  - Migration schedule (if migrations are performed in waves)
- Post migration surveys (especially when doing pilot migrations or waves of migrations)
- Building the hype! (People will embrace change if there is excitement in the air for it—distribute information, stand up kiosks for users to see what the experience is like, hang up posters or banners, create an Office 365 FAQ site, and so on)

Training is also an important focus area when performing a migration. This is less necessary for users moving from Exchange to Exchange Online. The time when it is, is when the users are changing Outlook clients or moving to use only **Outlook Web Apps (OWA)**. If an organization is moving from a non-Exchange messaging system, training is critical. Some areas you should consider for non-Exchange to Exchange Online training are:

- Distribute Outlook cheat sheets (quick reference guides)
- An in-class or virtual introduction training
- Sign up for an in-class or virtual power user training
- Video training posted on an Office 365 internal site
- Train power users or pilot users and have them walk the floors on go-live

There is certainly quite a bit of technical and business tasks to perform in order to prepare and execute a migration. Often times the users do not see these tasks occurring. What the user does see is how aware and ready they are for the migration to a new platform. The more time you spend on communications and training, the more likely you will have a successful migration.

Summary

By now we should have a good understanding on how to prepare Office 365 for the integration servers. Now, we should start to prepare our internal infrastructure for integration and think about how to prepare for the process. This preparation should guide us to start the initial integration and ready our pilot users to measure their experience within Office 365.

In the upcoming chapter, we will build the necessary integration components to prepare for our first migrations to Office 365.

8
Deploying a Hybrid Infrastructure: ADFS

Now that we have learned about the preparation requirements for integration, let's start to build the initial foundation that will enable us to prepare for integrated use and a migration to Office 365. By now, we should have the necessary physical or virtual servers, firewall, and DNS ready or in place. We will now focus on building three core services, enabled by Office 365. These core services are:

- Deploying **Active Directory Federation Services (ADFS)**
- Office 365 Directory Synchronization
- Exchange Hybrid

It's critical that we deploy these services in the order they are listed. If you choose to install these items out of order, some alternative configuration changes will be required and are not described. Currently they are listed in order, suggested by Microsoft best practices. In this chapter, we will focus on building ADFS with a **Windows Internal Database (WID)** as our database source (you may want to consider SQL for deployments requiring a larger scale).

In this chapter, we will look at the following topic:

- Deploying Active Directory Federation Services

Deploying Active Directory Federation Services

We are going to start by building the minimum requirements for ADFS. To do so, we will need one ADFS internal server and one ADFS proxy server. The ADFS internal server will be the primary ADFS server that manages the ADFS database on WID. The ADFS proxy server will refer to the ADFS internal server, when passing authentication. The servers should be prepared and placed according to the preparation requirements found in *Chapter 7, Preparing for a Hybrid Deployment and Migration*. Let's start by building the servers in the following order:

- Active Directory Federation Services internal server
- Active Directory Federation Services proxy server

Installing the Active Directory Federation Services internal server

The following high-level steps will be performed when installing the ADFS internal server:

- Installing ADFS
- Installing Office 365 Desktop Setup
- Installing Microsoft Online Services Module for Windows PowerShell
- Modifying the ADFS service
- Generating an ADFS certificate
- Configuring the ADFS internal server
- Converting the domain to a federated domain in Office 365

Installing ADFS

For this example, we are going to build the ADFS internal server with the following specifications:

- Windows Server 2008 R2 64-bit
- 4 GB of memory
- Quad core 2 GHz
- Active Directory joined
- All of the latest Windows Updates applied

- Computer name: ADFSINT (you will want to name this server based on your standard AD object naming scheme)

To start, let's make sure that we have the proper software located on the server:

- Download ADFS 2.0 RTW from the following URL:

  ```
  http://www.microsoft.com/download/en/details.
  aspx?displaylang=en&id=10909
  ```

  During the installation process, the following Windows components will be automatically installed:

  - Windows PowerShell
  - .NET Framework 3.5 SP1
  - **Internet Information Services (IIS)**
  - Windows Identity Foundation

- Download Update Rollup 1 for ADFS 2.0 from the following URL:

  ```
  http://support.microsoft.com/kb/2607496
  ```

- Download Microsoft Online Services Identity Federation Management Tool from the following URL:

  ```
  http://g.microsoftonline.com/0BD00en-US/126
  ```

Let's start with the ADFS installation:

1. Start the ADFS executable setup.
2. After launching the Setup wizard, click on **Next**:

3. If you accept the agreement, check the **I accept the terms in the Licence Agreement** checkbox, and click on **Next**:

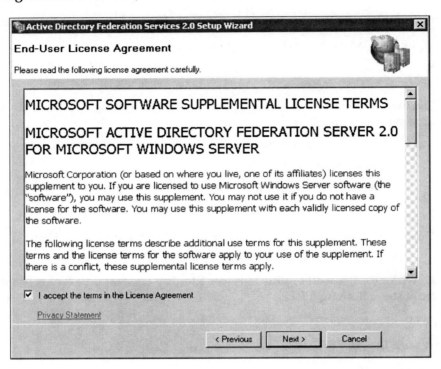

4. Select **Federation Server** and click on **Next**:

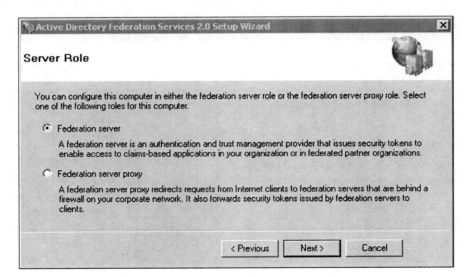

5. The wizard will attempt to install all the necessary prerequisites. Click on **Next**:

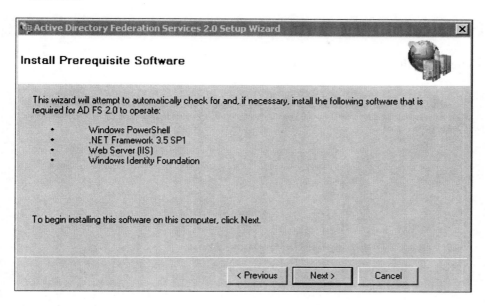

6. At this point, continue to monitor the installation until all prerequisites and ADFS are installed:

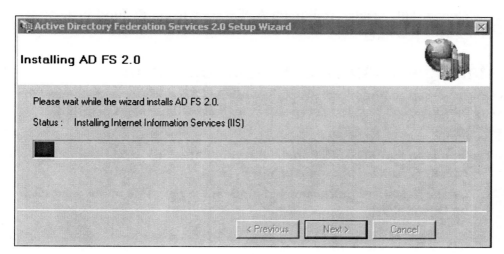

7. When the installation is complete, uncheck the **Start the ADFS Management snap-in when this wizard closes** checkbox. Click on **Finish**:

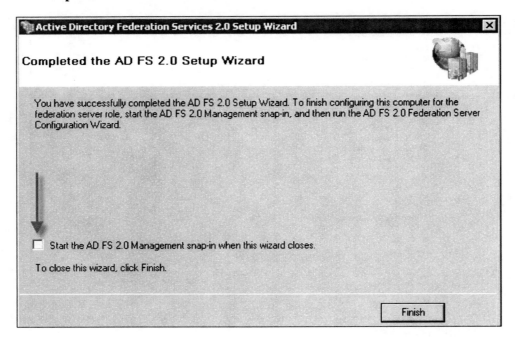

8. Now install the latest roll-up for ADFS. We will use Rollup 1 in our installation, as mentioned in the preceding download list.

Installing the Office 365 Desktop Setup

To ensure we can communicate properly with the Office 365 service, we need to deploy the Office 365 Desktop Setup software. Follow these steps to install the software:

1. Sign in to the Office 365 Portal, with your Office 365 admin account at `https://portal.microsoftonline.com`

2. On the **Resources** quick launch, found on the right side of the page, click on **Downloads**:

3. On the Downloads page, move to step 3 and click on **Set up**:

4. You may be prompted with a security warning. Click on **Run**:

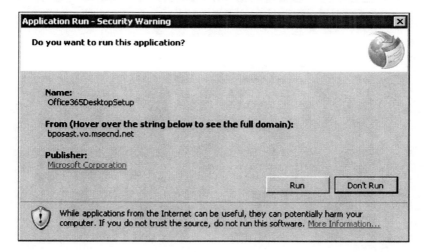

5. If you receive another logon prompt, enter the same admin credentials you used to log on to the Office 365 Portal.

6. This will bring up the Desktop updates screen. This will list **Microsoft Online Services Sign-in Assistant**, which is a requirement for the upcoming Federation Management tool. Uncheck any options that may be checked in the **Select applications to configure** section. Click on **Continue**:

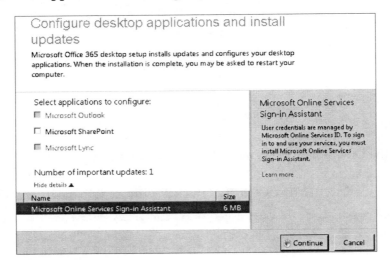

7. The software update will now begin. If you accept the agreement, click on **I accept**:

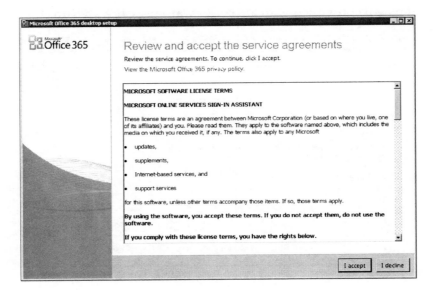

8. Click on **Finish** to complete the installation:

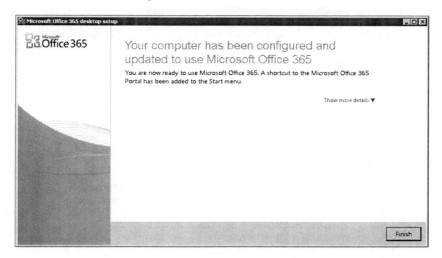

Installing the Microsoft Online Services Module for Windows PowerShell

We need to run PowerShell commands to establish the trust. Follow these steps to simplify running these PowerShell commands:

1. Download and launch `AdministrationConfig-en.msi`. This file (64-bit version) can be downloaded from `http://g.microsoftonline.com/0BD00en-US/126`. Click on **Next**:

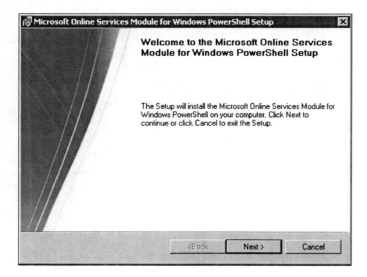

2. If you accept the agreement, check the **I accept the terms in the License Terms** checkbox and click on **Next**:

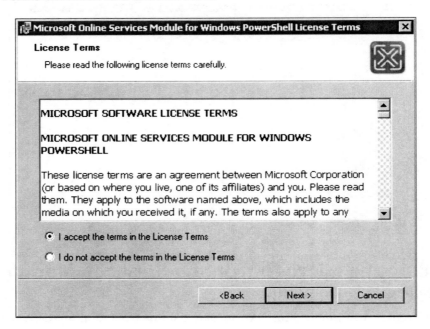

3. In the next screen, accept the default path and click on **Next**:

4. Now click on **Install**:

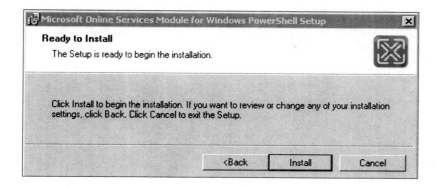

5. Finish the installation by clicking on **Finish**.

Modifying the ADFS service

Let's now set the ADFS admin account, created previously to the ADFS 2.0 Windows Service.

1. Open the Services management console (`services.msc`) and locate **ADFS 2.0 Windows Service**:

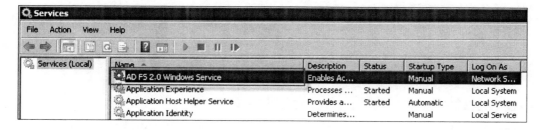

2. Go to the properties of this service and click on the **Log On** tab.

3. Change the **Log on as** account to your ADFS admin account and click on **OK**:

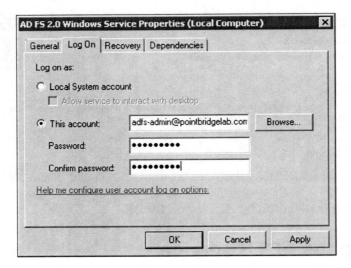

4. Now click on **OK**:

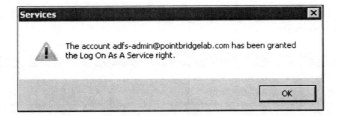

Generating an ADFS certificate

Before configuring ADFS, we need to create a **Certificate Signing Request (CSR)** and purchase the third-party certificate for sts.yourdomain.com. In this example, we will use sts.pointbridgelab.com.

In order to create and assign the certificate properly, we will follow this approach:

- Create and complete a CSR
- Add the ADFS service account to the certificate

Creating and completing a CSR

In the following steps, we will create the CSR from the ADFS server and apply it:

1. Open Internet Information Services (IIS) Manager on the ADFS server, found under **Administrative Tools** in the **Start** menu.

2. Click on the server name and open the **Server Certificates** window:

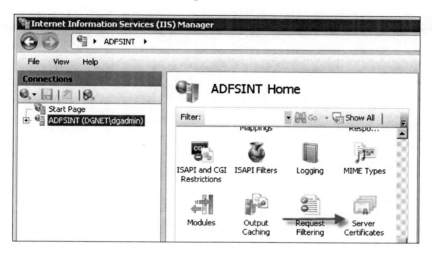

3. Click on **Create Certificate Request** in the **Actions** pane, found on the right side:

4. Fill the form using the FQDN name you wish to use for your federation website. An example is as follows, based on the preparation guide. Click on **Next**:

   ° **Common name: sts.pointbridgelab.com**

   ° **Organization: PointBridge Lab**

   ° **Organizational unit: Information Technology**

- ° **City/locality**: Chicago
- ° **State/province**: IL
- ° **Country/region**: US

The following screenshot shows the **Request Certificate** form with these details filled in:

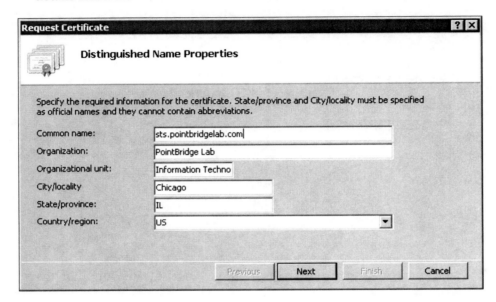

5. Select **Microsoft RSA SChannel Cryptographic Provider** and a bit length of **2048**. Click on **Next**:

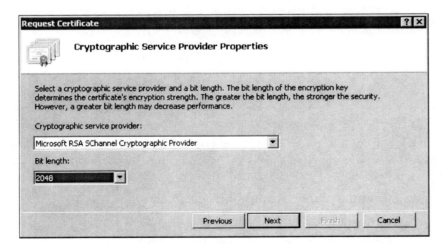

6. Enter the name for the request file and click on **Finish**:

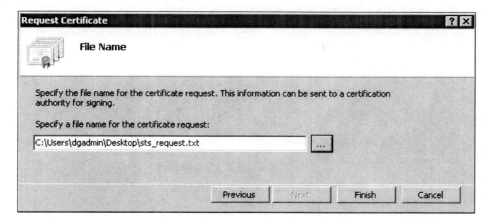

7. Connect to your public CA and paste the contents of the request file into the form or attach the file.

8. When you receive the certificate you'll need to finish processing the request. Open Internet Information Services (IIS) Manager on the ADFS server and navigate back to the Server Certificates view and click on **Complete Certificate Request...** in the **Actions** pane:

9. Locate the file you received from the CA and give it a friendly name and click on **OK**. In this example, our friendly name would be **sts.pointbridgelab.com**:

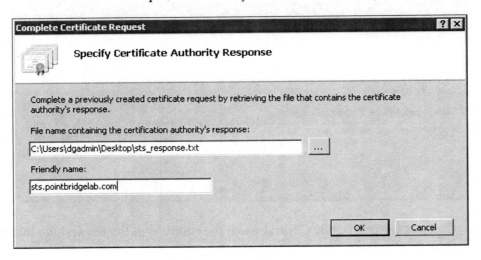

10. You should now see the new certificate listed:

11. Next, you need to assign this certificate to the default website. Click on **Default Web Site** and then click on **Bindings...** in the **Actions** pane:

12. Click on **Add...** in the **Site Bindings** page:

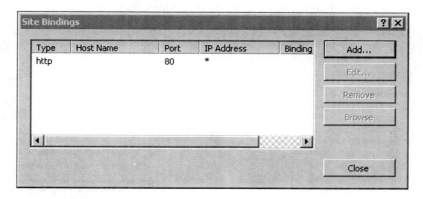

13. Select **https** from the **Type** drop-down menu. Select the new certificate from the **SSL certificate** drop-down menu and make sure that the port is **443**. Click on **OK**. Close the window to save the settings:

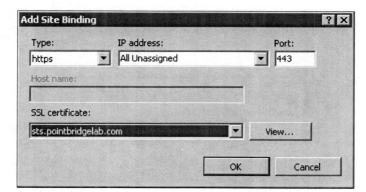

Adding the ADFS service account to the certificate

The ADFS service account should have permissions to the certificate. Follow these steps to assign permissions to the certificate:

1. On the ADFS server, open MMC by entering **mmc** in the **Run** window. Add the **Certificates** snap-in under the Computer account, then local computer.

2. Locate the certificate you installed under **Personal** | **Certificates**. Right-click on the certificate and click on **Manage Private Keys...**:

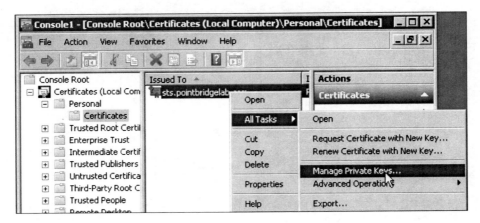

3. Add the **ADFS Admin** service account with **Read** access. Click on **OK**:

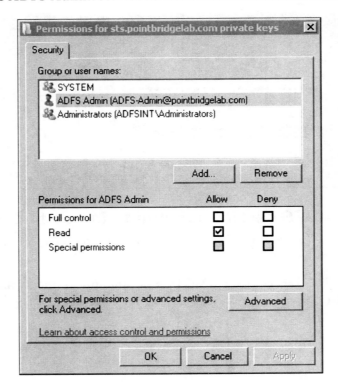

4. Finally, perform a `iisreset /noforce` operation from an administrative command prompt:

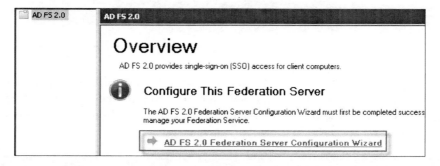

Configuring the ADFS internal server

Now that all of our initial preparation steps are complete, let's start to configure the ADFS internal server by following these steps:

1. Open ADFS Management 2.0 Wizard from the **Start** | **Administrative Tools**.

2. Click on **AD FS 2.0 Federation Server Configuration Wizard**:

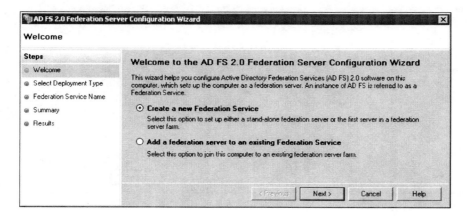

3. Select **Create a new Federation Service**. Click on **Next**:

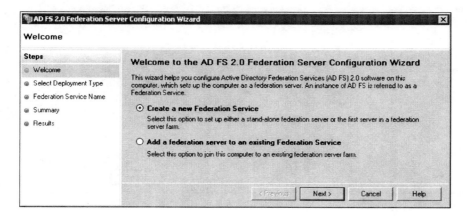

4. This will be the first server in the federation farm, select **New federation server farm**. Click on **Next**:

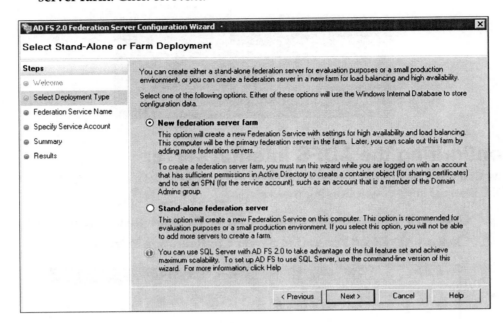

5. Verify that the SSL certificate, **sts.yourdomain.com** (this example will be `sts.pointbridgelab.com`) is selected, and that the Federation Service name matches the name of the certificate. After verifying these settings, click on **Next**:

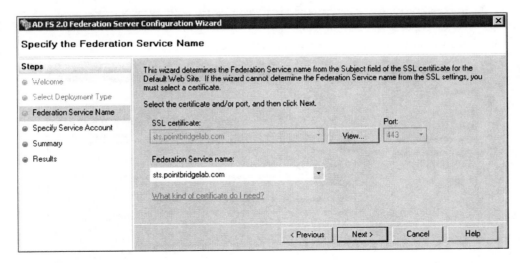

6. Browse to locate the **ADFS-Admin** service account and then provide the password for the service account. Click on **Next** to continue:

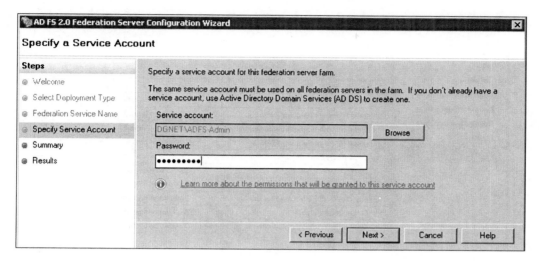

7. Review the summary and click on **Next** when ready to start the installation:

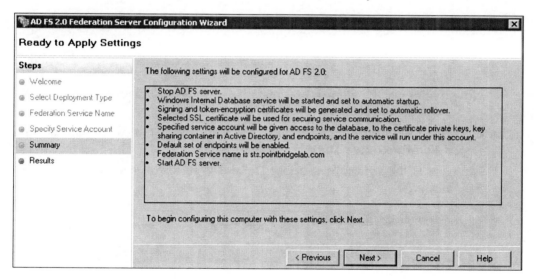

8. This will begin the installation of ADFS components on the server. The **Close** option will become available when all components complete successfully:

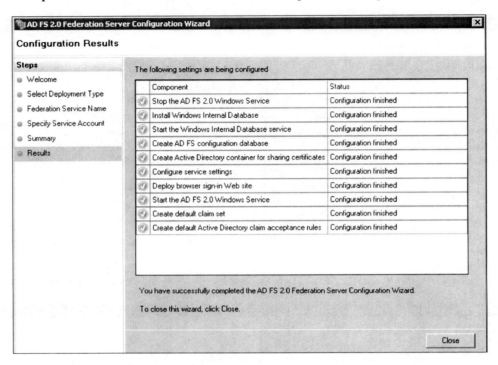

9. Now that the ADFS database is created and an IIS ADFS website exists, let's go back to IIS and set the proper SSL requirements.

10. Open Internet Information Services (IIS) Manager on the ADFS server found under **Administrative Tools** in the **Start** menu.

11. Navigate to the **adfs** subsite under **Default Web Site** and select **SSL Settings**:

12. If not already accepted, enable the **Require SSL** setting and select **Accept** under **Client certificates**. Click on **Apply** in the upper-right pane:

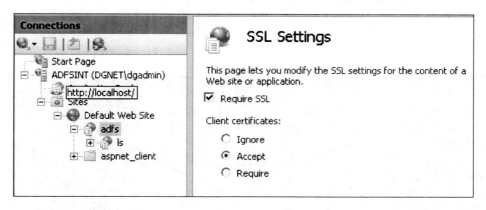

Converting the domain to a federated domain in Office 365

We will now federate the `pointbridgelab.com` domain within the Office 365 service. To do this, follow these steps:

1. Open Microsoft Online Services Module for Windows PowerShell on the ADFS internal server, as an administrator. Use your Office 365 admin credentials at the pop-up prompt for credentials.

2. Enter **set-ExecutionPolicy unrestricted**. This command allows you to run commands with elevated privileges.

3. Enter **$cred=get-credential**. This command allows you to enter your Office 365 administration account credentials when prompted to login.

4. Enter **Connect-MsolService -Credential $cred**. This command connects you to your Office 365 service.

5. Enter **Set-MsolADFSContext -computer ADFSINT**. This command replaces **ADFSINT** with your ADFS Server name.

6. Enter **Convert-MsolDomainToFederated –DomainName pointbridgelab. com**. This command replaces **pointbridgelab.com** with your domain.

7. Enter **Update-MSOLFederatedDomain -domainname pointbridgelab.com**. This command updates Office 365 with your ADFS server information.

If you need to add support for multiple domains, you will need to add the -SupportMultipleDomain switch to the Convert and Update cmdlets. For more details on support for multiple domains, visit http://community.office365.com/en-us/w/sso/support-for-multiple-top-level-domains.aspx.

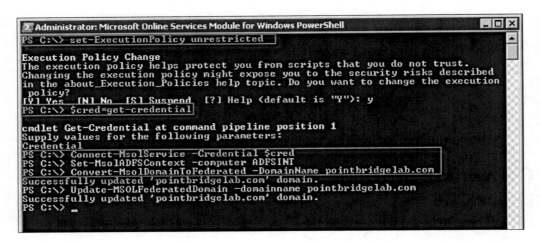

8. To determine if federation has been enabled, enter Get-MSOLFederationProperty -DomainName pointbridgelab.com in the command prompt. You can also check in the portal to determine if federation is enabled. If the domain is listed as a **Single sign-on** type, the domain is set properly:

Installing Active Directory Federation Services proxy server

The following high-level steps will be performed during the installation of the ADFS proxy server:

- Installing ADFS
- Installing Office 365 Desktop Setup
- Editing hosts files
- Modifying the ADFS service
- Importing the ADFS certificate
- Configuring the ADFS proxy server

Installing ADFS

For this example, we are going to build the ADFS proxy server with the following specifications:

- Windows Server 2008 R2 64-bit
- 4 GB of memory
- Quad core 2 GHz
- Does not have to be Active Directory joined
- All of the latest Windows updates applied
- User Access Control is turned off
- Computer name: ADFSPROXY (you will want to name this server based on your standard AD object naming scheme)
- Deployed in DMZ - HTTPS (TCP 443) required to be open between the proxy server and the internal ADFS server and also required from the Internet to the ADFS proxy server
- Using the SSL certificate from the primary internal ADFS server, imported through IIS

To start, let's make sure we have the proper software located on the server:

- Download ADFS 2.0 RTW from the following URL:

  `http://www.microsoft.com/download/en/details.`
  `aspx?displaylang=en&id=10909`

  During the installation process, the following Windows components will be automatically installed:

  - Windows PowerShell
  - .NET Framework 3.5 SP1
  - Internet Information Services (IIS)
  - Windows Identity Foundation

- Download Update Rollup 1 for ADFS 2.0 from the following URL:

  `http://support.microsoft.com/kb/2607496`

Let's start with the ADFS installation:

1. If your computer is not domain joined, you need to create a local user account with administrative privileges and then log on with that account for all installations. (In this example, we created an account called **ADFS-Proxy**).

2. Start the ADFS executable setup.

3. After launching the Setup wizard, click on **Next**:

4. If you accept the agreement, click on **Next**:

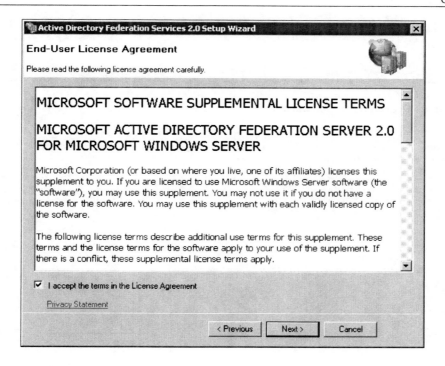

5. Now select **Federation server proxy** and click on **Next**:

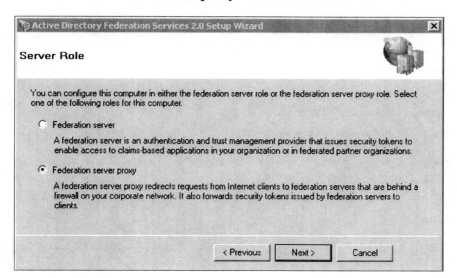

6. The wizard will attempt to install all the necessary prerequisites. Click on **Next**:

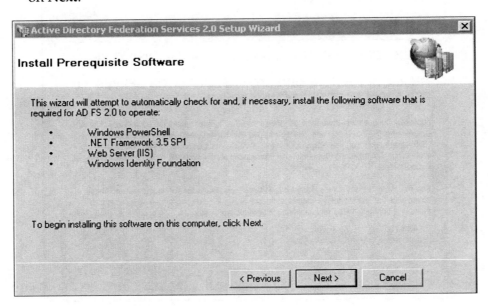

7. At this point, continue to monitor the installation until all of the prerequisites and ADFS are installed:

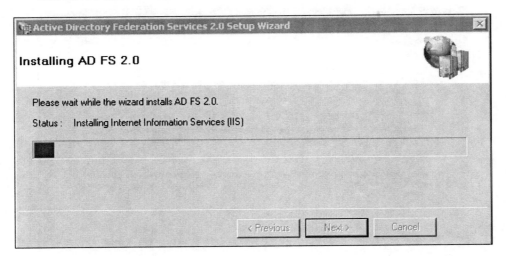

8. When the installation is complete, uncheck **Start the ADFS Management snap-in when this wizard closes**. Click on **Finish**:

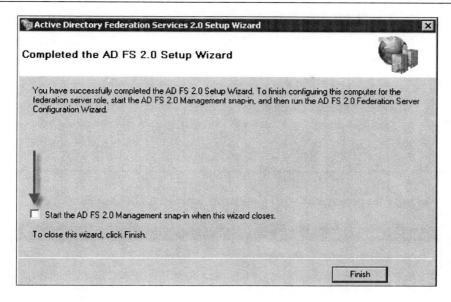

9. Now install the latest rollup for ADFS. We will use Rollup 1 in our installation.

Installing the Office 365 Desktop Setup

To ensure we can communicate properly with the Office 365 service, we need to deploy the Office 365 Desktop Setup software. Follow these steps to install the software:

1. Sign in to the Office 365 Portal, with your Office 365 admin account at `https://portal.microsoftonline.com`.

2. On the **Resources** quick launch, found on the right side of the page, click on **Downloads**:

3. On the downloads page, skip to step 3 and click on **Set up**:

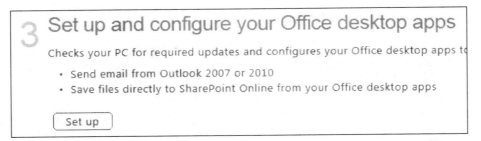

4. You may be prompted with a security warning, click on **Run**:

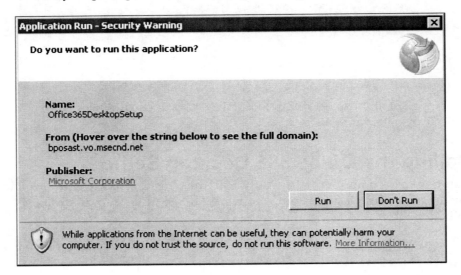

5. If you receive another logon prompt, enter the same admin credentials you used to log on to the Office 365 Portal.

6. This will bring up the desktop updates screen. This will list the **Microsoft Online Services Sign-in Assistant**, which is a requirement for the upcoming Federation Management tool. Uncheck any options that may be checked in the **Select applications to configure** section. Click on **Continue**:

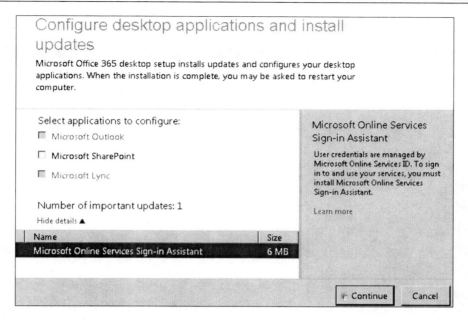

7. The software update will now begin. If you accept the agreement, click on **I accept**:

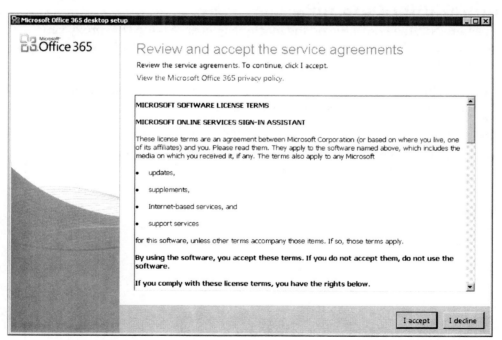

8. Click on **Finish** to complete the installation:

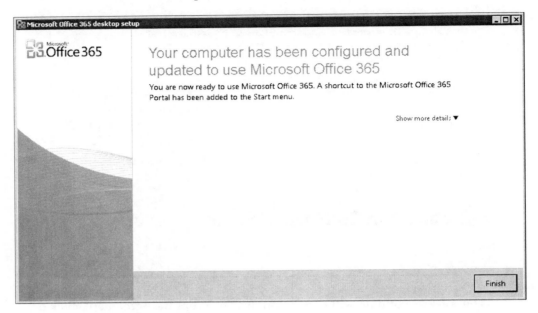

Editing the hosts file

We need to edit the `hosts` file on the machine to ensure the ADFS proxy can communicate with the ADFS internal and not rely on external DNS entries. To do this, follow these steps:

1. Edit the `hosts` file and add an entry to resolve the federation server's URL to the internal IP address of the internal.

 External users should be directed to your ADFS proxy, when reaching `sts.yourdomain.com`.

2. To edit the `hosts` file, open Notepad as an administrator and find the `hosts` file under `C:\Windows\System32\drivers\etc`:

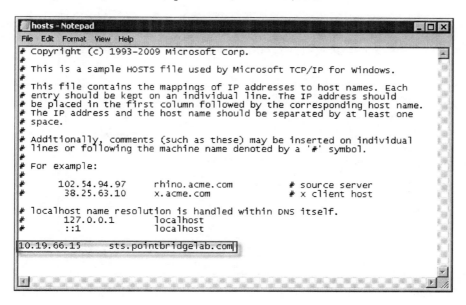

Modifying the ADFS service

Let's now set the ADFS-Proxy account, previously created to log on to the ADFS Proxy server:

1. Open the Service Management console (`services.msc`) and locate **ADFS 2.0 Windows Service**:

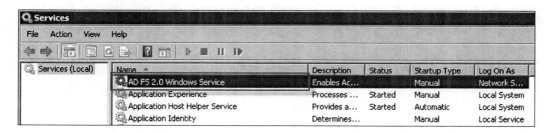

2. Go to the properties of this service and then click on the **Log On** tab.

3.   Change the **Log on as** account to your ADFS-Proxy account, then click on OK:

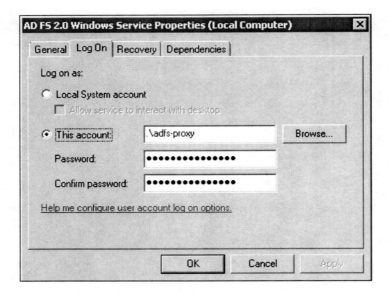

4.   Now click on **OK**:

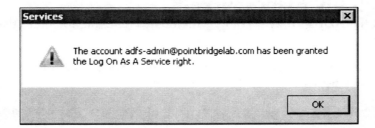

Importing the ADFS certificate

Users will be accessing the ADFS proxy and will require secure communications. Follow these steps to apply the ADFS proxy certificate:

1.   Export the certificate as a PFX file from your ADFS internal server. Ensure that the private key is included.

2.   Open Internet Information Services (IIS) Manager on the ADFS server found under **Administrative Tools** in the **Start** menu.

3. Click on the server name and open the **Server Certificates** window:

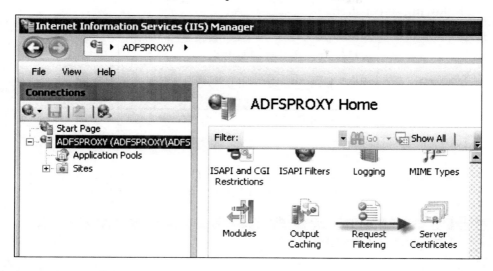

4. Click on **Import** in the **Action Pane**, found on the right side:

5. Locate the exported certificate file and click on **OK**:

6. You should now see the new certificate listed, as shown in the following screenshot:

7. Next, you need to assign this certificate to **Default Web Site**. Navigate to **Default Web Site** and click on **Bindings...** in the **Actions** pane:

8. Click on **Add...** in the **Site Bindings** page:

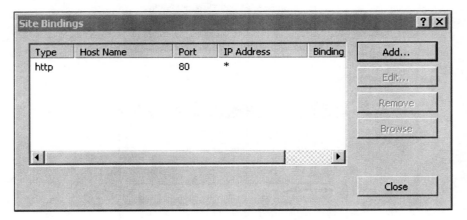

9. Select **https** from the **Type** drop-down menu and select the new certificate from the list and make sure the port is **443**. Click on **OK** and close the window to save the settings:

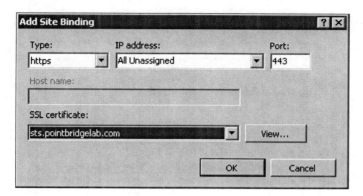

Adding the ADFS service account to the certificate

We need to ensure that the ADFS service account can access the certificate successfully. Follow these steps to assign the service account permissions to the certificate.

1. In the ADFS server, open the MMC (enter **mmc** in the **Run** prompt) and add the **Certificates** snap-in under the computer account, then under local computer.

2. Locate the certificate you installed under the **Personal | Certificates** store. Right-click on the certificate and select **Manage Private Keys...**.

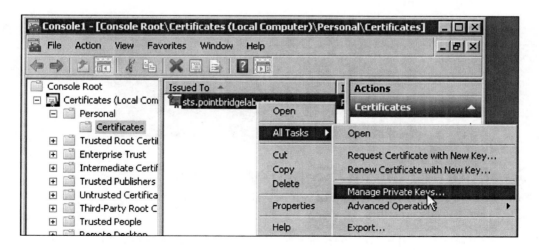

3. Add the **ADFS-Proxy** account with **Read** access. Click on **OK**:

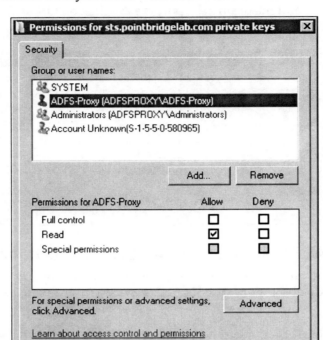

4. Finally, perform a `iisreset/noforce` operation from an administrative command prompt:

Configuring the ADFS proxy server

Now that we have completed all of our preparation requirements, let's begin the ADFS proxy configuration:

1. Open the ADFS 2.0 Federation Server Proxy Configuration Wizard from the **Start** menu, found under **Administrative Tools**. Click on **Next**, to get started:

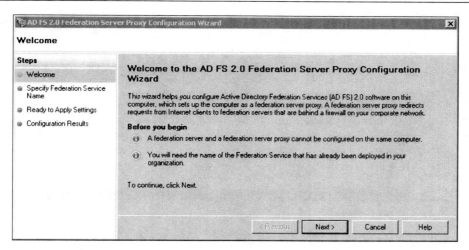

2. Enter the federation service name, `sts.yourdomain.com` (in this example, it is **sts.pointbridgelab.com**) and click on **Test Connection**:

 If this step fails, check your `hosts` file or firewall rules to ensure traffic can get through.

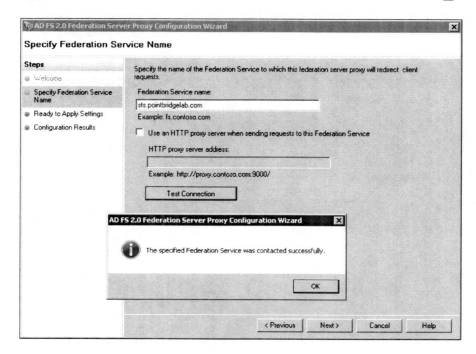

3. Click on **Next**. Enter the credentials that will be used to establish the trust. Enter the domain account ADFS-Auth created in *Chapter 7, Preparing for a Hybrid Deployment and Migration*. Click on **OK**.

 If you receive an error, double check and ensure that the ADFS-Auth account is a local admin on the ADFS internal server.

4. Now click on **Next** to apply the ADFS settings:

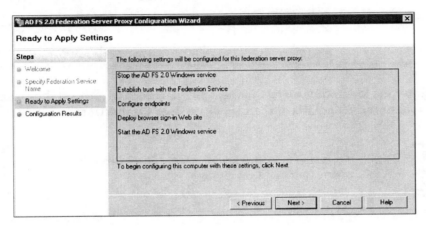

5. Once the configuration completes, click on **Close**.

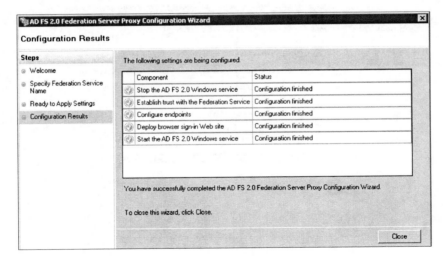

6. This concludes the configuration requirements for the ADFS proxy server.

Summary

In this chapter we learned how to build the first core integration point ADFS to support authentication services with Office 365.

In our next chapter, we will focus on the build out of Directory Synchronization, which is a critical component to the ADFS authentication. Directory Synchronization allows us to leverage the ADFS deployment by synchronizing and informing the service about who is federated and who is not.

9
Deploying a Hybrid Infrastructure: Directory Synchronization

Now that we have deployed Active Directory Federation Services (ADFS), let's start to build out our next core service—Directory Synchronization. By now, you should have the necessary physical or virtual servers ready or in place. As mentioned in *Chapter 8*, *Deploying a Hybrid Infrastructure: ADFS*, Directory Synchronization is the second service we need to build for our Office 365 integration.

In this chapter, we will look at the following topic:

- Deploying Directory Synchronization

Deploying Directory Synchronization

After both the ADFS internal and ADFS proxy servers are installed and configured, we need to start the installation of Directory Synchronization, before we can start testing whether ADFS was set up successfully. The following high-level steps will be performed when installing the Directory Synchronization server:

- Confirming the preparation specifications
- Enabling and downloading Directory Synchronization
- Installing Directory Synchronization
- Configuring Directory Synchronization

Confirming the preparation specifications

For this example, we are going to build the Directory Synchronization server with the following specifications:

- Windows Server 2008 R2 64-bit
- 4 GB of memory
- Quad core 2 GHz
- Active Directory joined
- All of the latest Windows Updates applied
- Computer Name—DIRSYNC (you will want to name this server based on your standard AD object naming scheme)
- There is a 10,000 object limit for Directory Synchronization but this can be increased by opening a service request with Office 365 support.
- SQL Server 2008 Express (An external SQL server may be necessary, based on the objects' sync requirements. These requirements can be found here at `http://onlinehelp.microsoft.com/en-us/Office365-enterprises/ff652544.aspx`.)

Installing the Directory Synchronization tool creates the `MSOL_AD_SYNC` account in the standard Users organizational unit of the local Active Directory. This account is used by the Directory Synchronization tool to read the local Active Directory information. Do not move or remove this account. Moving or removing this account will cause synchronization failures.

Enabling and downloading Directory Synchronization

We first need to start out by enabling the service within Office 365 and downloading the initial software. This is a necessary step to start the Directory Synchronization process.

1. From the Directory Synchronization server, log in to the Office 365 Admin Portal using an account with Global Admin credentials (`https://portal.microsoftonline.com/admin`).

2. Locate the **Management** section on the left-hand side of the screen and click on **Users**:

3. Click on **Set up** next to **Active Directory synchronization**.

4. Click on **Activate** under **step 3**. Now click on **Activate** in the dialogue box that appears:

5. Now, download the 64-bit version of Directory Synchronization:

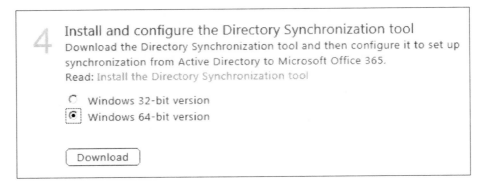

Installing Directory Synchronization

We will now install the Directory Synchronization software, in preparation to configure our first synchronization to Office 365.

1. Launch the Directory Synchronization setup as an administrator and click on **Next**:

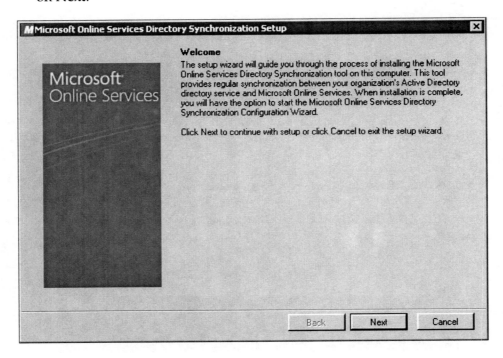

2. The next screen will display the Microsoft Software License Terms. If you agree with the terms, accept the agreement and click on **Next**:

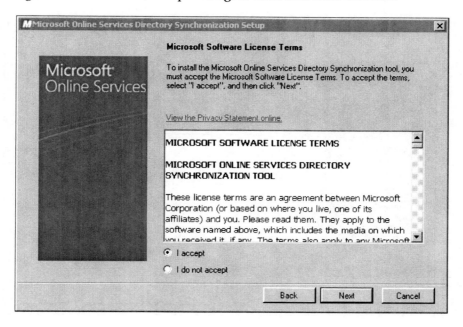

3. Click on **Next** with the default installation directory selected:

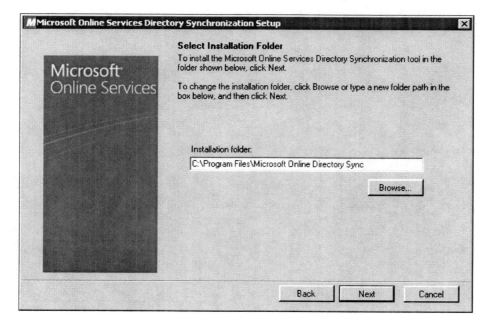

4. The installation may take some time. When the status bar is complete, click on **Next**:

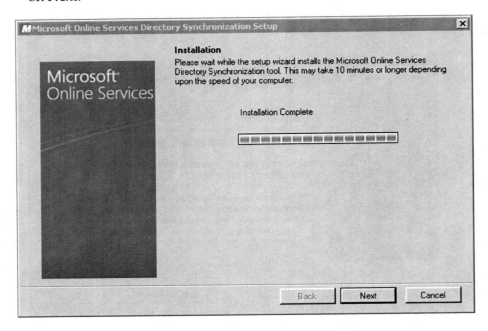

5. Uncheck the **Start Configuration Wizard now** checkbox and click on **Finish**:

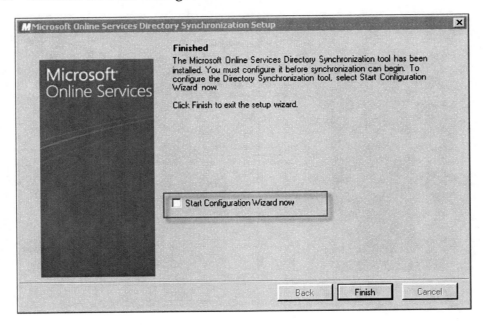

Configuring Directory Synchronization

Now that Directory Synchronization is installed, let's start the configuration for our first synchronization. To do this, follow these steps:

1. Launch the desktop shortcut for the Directory Synchronization wizard and click on **Next**:

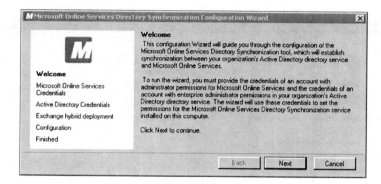

2. On the **Microsoft Online Services Credentials** page, enter your Microsoft Online Services Administrator Credentials and click on **Next**:

 You may want to create a new account in the Office 365 admin portal, exclusive for this service. Creating a separate account and excluding it from your default password policy, will prevent Directory Synchronization from halting, due to an expired account.

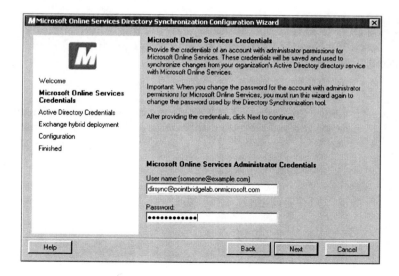

3. On the Active Directory Credentials page, enter your Active Directory Enterprise Admin Credentials and click on **Next**:

 Ensure that you have also logged on to this computer with the same credential and that account is a member of the local MIISAdmins group. If not, you may receive a registry write error.

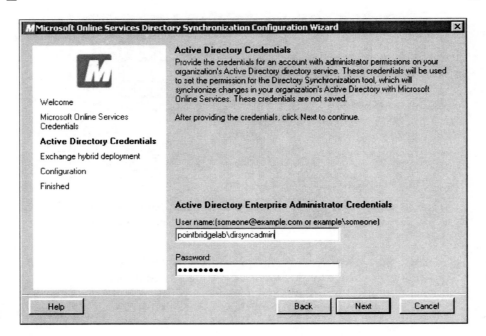

4. Our objective is to take full advantage of the migration capabilities to Office 365. Check the **Enable Exchange hybrid deployment** checkbox and click on **Next**:

 Enabling the Exchange Hybrid deployment allows you to share information and migrate mailboxes to and from Office 365.

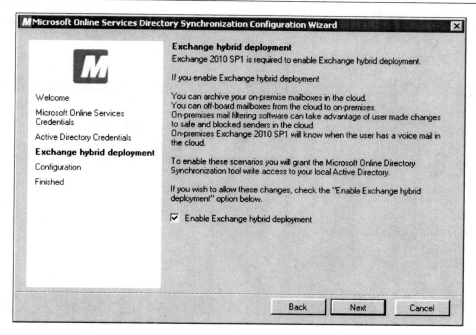

5. Once the configuration is complete, click on **Next**:

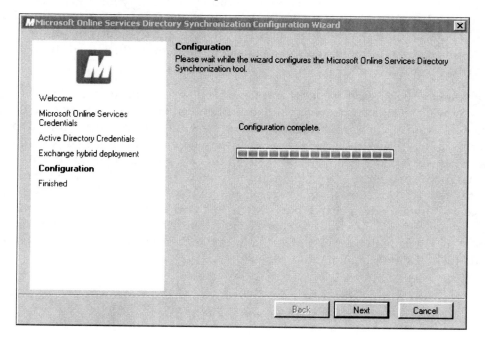

6. When we finish the configuration, the last step is to close the configuration wizard and start Directory Synchronization. To close the wizard, click on **Finish**:

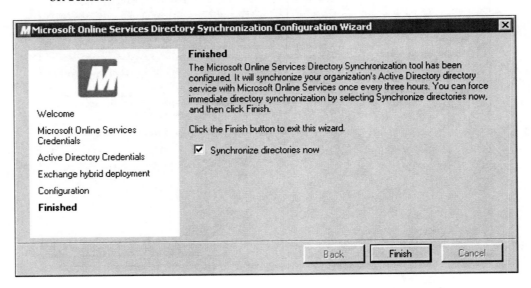

Directory Synchronization should now be running. Based on your organization size, this could take a few minutes to a few hours. Check the Office 365 Admin portal, to see if your accounts have synchronized. If after 24 hours you do not see the synchronized accounts, you may have to troubleshoot for conflicts or restrictions in the environment.

Once you have confirmed accounts and have been synchronized to Office 365, you may want to take this time to validate authentication works properly. To do so, just take one of your synchronized accounts in Office 365 and try to log on to `https://portal.microsoftonilne.com`. After you enter the user's UPN logon (`%username%@domain.com`), you should get either a logon dialog from your ADFS internal server or a forms-based logon from your ADFS proxy. After you log on with the user's Active Directory logon credentials (UPN), you should either receive the message — **You are not licensed to use Microsoft Office 365**, or you will be provided with options that your account has been enabled with. Either way, if logging on from within your network and outside your network produce the same results, you should be in a good shape to move forward.

If you do not receive a logon dialog from the internal ADFS server or a forms-based logon from your ADFS proxy, you may need to troubleshoot to find out why the authentication is not working. Most commonly, authentication generally does not work properly when Firewall rules are not specified properly, DNS records are not created properly, or the install of ADFS and Directory Synchronization did not complete successfully.

Summary

In this chapter we learned how to build the second core integration point, Directory Synchronization, to support authentication services, address book synchronization, and the future deployment of Exchange Hybrid with Office 365.

In our next chapter, we will focus on building out Exchange Hybrid, which is a critical component of our migration to Exchange Online from Exchange on-premise.

10

Deploying a Hybrid Infrastructure: Exchange Hybrid

Now that we have deployed Directory Synchronization, let's start to configure our next core service, Exchange Hybrid. By now, you should have the necessary physical or virtual servers, firewall, and DNS ready or in place. As mentioned in *Chapter 8, Deploying a Hybrid Infrastructure: ADFS*, Exchange Hybrid is the third service we need to build for our Office 365 integration.

In this chapter, we will look at the following topic:

- Deploying Exchange Hybrid

Deploying Exchange Hybrid

By now, ADFS and Directory Synchronization should be deployed and tested. Do not proceed with Exchange Hybrid, unless Directory Synchronization has fully synchronized your environment. The following high-level steps will be performed when installing the Exchange Hybrid:

- Confirming preparation specifications
- Preparing the Exchange 2010 Server
- Creating a Hybrid configuration
- Configuring the Hybrid configuration

Confirming preparation specifications

We will assume that you have already deployed an Exchange 2010 SP2 server within your environment. It should meet the following requirements:

- Exchange 2010 Service Pack 2 deployed, with at least the Client Access Server and Hub Transport Server roles deployed

- Existing Exchange versions within the same Exchange Organization can communicate properly with the Exchange 2010 server deployed

- The Exchange 2010 server is externally accessible

- The Exchange 2010 server has a well-known public certificate for Autodiscover and **Exchange Web Services (EWS)**

Preparing Exchange 2010 Server

As we prepare to create the Hybrid configuration, we need to ensure the Exchange 2010 server can connect properly to the Office 365 service. In order to achieve this, we need to deploy the Office 365 Desktop Setup on the Exchange 2010 server and add the Office 365 subscription as an additional Exchange Forest, within the Exchange Management Console.

Installing the Office 365 Desktop Setup

To ensure proper communication with the Office 365 service, we need to deploy the Office 365 Desktop Setup software. Follow these steps to install the software:

1. Sign in to the Office 365 Portal, with your Office 365 admin account at `https://portal.microsoftonline.com`.

2. On the **Resources** quick launch, found on the right side of the page, click on **Downloads** (see the following screenshot):

3. On the Downloads page, move to step 3 and click on **Set Up**:

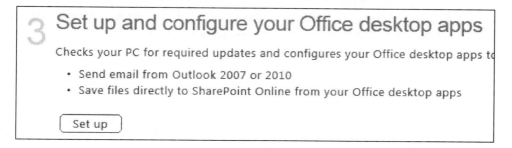

4. You may be prompted with a security warning. Click on **Run**:

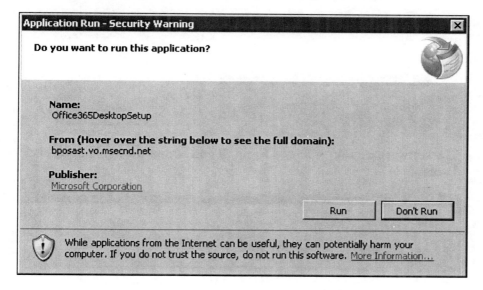

5. If you receive another logon prompt, enter the same admin credentials you used to log on to the Office 365 Portal.

6. This will bring up the Desktop updates screen. This screen will list **Microsoft Online Services Sign-in Assistant**, which is a requirement for the upcoming Federation Management tool. Uncheck any options that may be checked in the **Select applications to configure** section. Click on **Continue**:

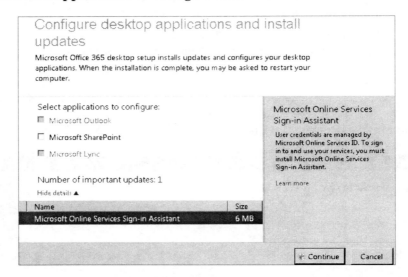

7. The software update will now begin. If you accept the agreement, click on **I accept**:

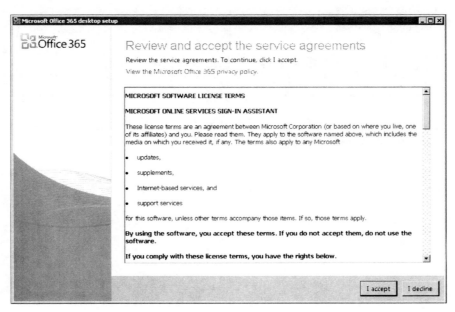

8. Click on **Finish** to complete the installation:

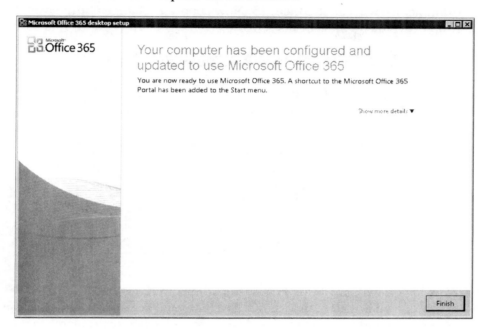

Adding your Office 365 subscription to the Exchange Management Console

The management interface for Office 365 should be added to Exchange 2010. The benefits of adding your Office 365 subscription to the **Exchange Management Console (EMC)** include ease of migrations, simplified management of your subscription, and provisioning of accounts. Let's add the Office 365 Exchange Organization; follow these steps:

1. Open the Exchange Management Console and then right-click on **Microsoft Exchange**. Click on **Add Exchange Forest...**:

2. Now, add a name for the Exchange forest that is easily identifiable. In this example, we will call it **Office 365**. Now choose **Exchange Online** from the drop-down menu and click on **OK**:

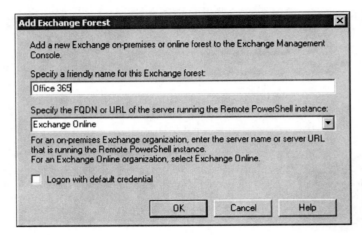

3. Now log on with an Office 365 Global Admin account. Try not to use a synchronized account (also known as a federated account). Doing this can help us to avoid troubleshooting ADFS versus Exchange problems that may come up. If you use a federated account, you could be troubleshooting two issues, if federation is really the only issue. Once you have entered your credentials, click on **OK**:

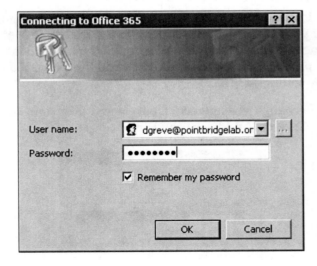

4. You should now see your Office 365 subscription in the Exchange Management Console:

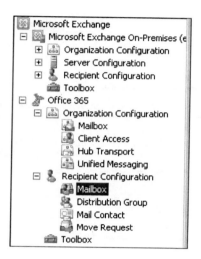

Creating a Hybrid configuration

At this point we should now be prepared to create the Hybrid Configuration by running the **New Hybrid Configuration** wizard. To do this, simply follow these steps:

1. In the Exchange Management Console, click on the on-premise **Organization Configuration**. In the Actions pane, click on **New Hybrid Configuration**:

2. As this will be the first Hybrid configuration, click on **New** to create the federation trust and a self-signed certificate:

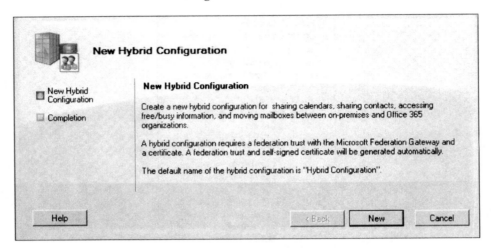

3. Once this step is complete, click on **Finish**:

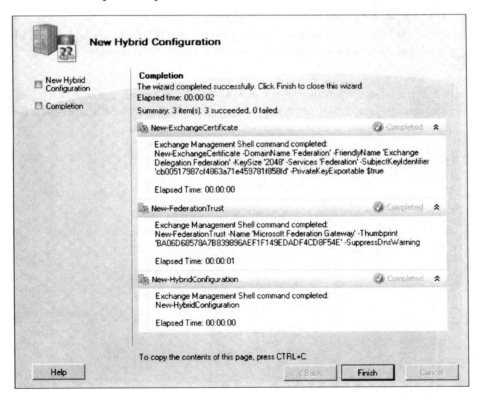

Configuring the Hybrid configuration

At this point, we now need to configure the Hybrid configuration between your Exchange Organization and Office 365. To do so, we will need a local account with Domain Admin and Exchange Organization admin privileges. In addition, we will need an Office 365 Global Admin account. You may want to create new accounts specifically for this purpose, or use existing accounts in both systems.

1. In the Exchange Management Console, click on the local Exchange Organization and highlight the Hybrid configuration. In the Actions pane, click on **Manage Hybrid Configuration**:

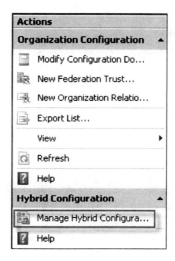

2. Click on **Next** in the **Introduction** screen.

3. Now enter your local account name with both Domain Admin and Exchange Organization Admin privileges and check the **Remember my credentials** checkbox. Next, enter your Office 365 Global Admin account name and check the **Remember my credentials** checkbox. Try to avoid using an ADFS enabled Global Admin account as this may cause you to have to take additional troubleshooting steps, if ADFS is not functioning properly. Click on **Next**:

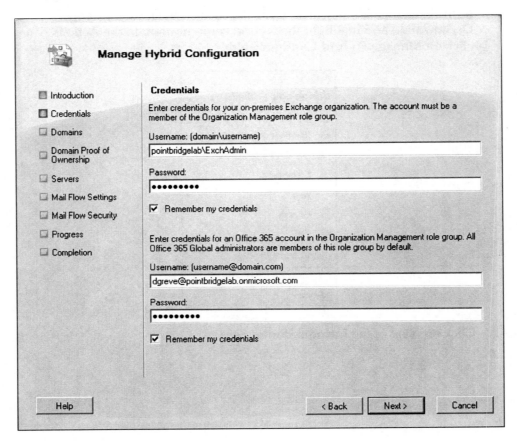

4. On the Domains page, click on **Add** and select all the domains that will be used with Office 365. Click on **Next**:

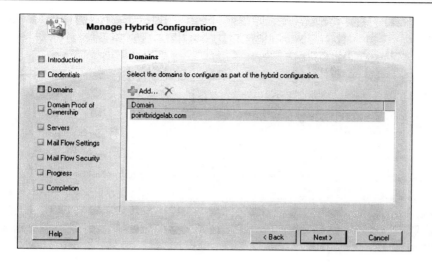

5. On the **Domain Proof of Ownership** screen, copy the contents and create an external DNS record. Once created and verified, check the **Check to confirm that the TXT records have been created in public DNS for the domains above** checkbox. Click on **Next**:

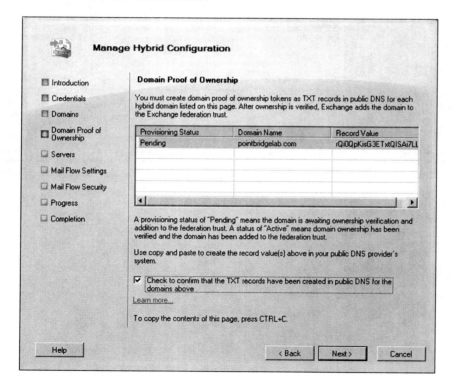

6. Let's now add the servers that will be managing the free/busy lookups, mailbox moves, and mail flow between the environments. In our example, we will only have one Exchange Hybrid server. Click on **Next**:

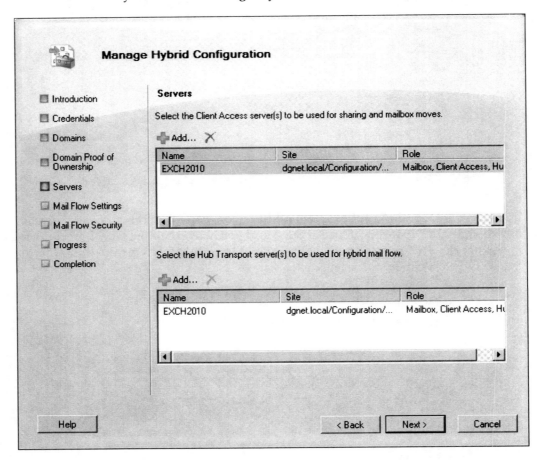

7. Now enter the externally accessible IP address and name for this Hybrid server. Click on **Next:**

 If you have not opened the firewall ports or assigned a record in DNS for your Hybrid server, be sure to do this now, based on the guidance provided in *Chapter 7, Preparing for a Hybrid Deployment and Migration.*

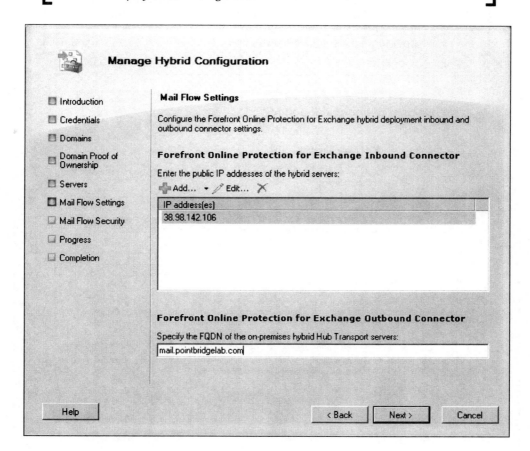

8. At this point, if you installed your certificate properly, it should automatically be listed. If you have more than one certificate, make sure you select the proper one. You also now have an option on how you would like to route mail traffic. For this example, we will have Office 365 route all outbound traffic for Office 365 users. Click on **Next**:

 You may want to route through your on-premise mail system, for compliance reasons, maintaining existing banner messages or to control on-premise routing rules — if you have not already pushed them to Office 365.

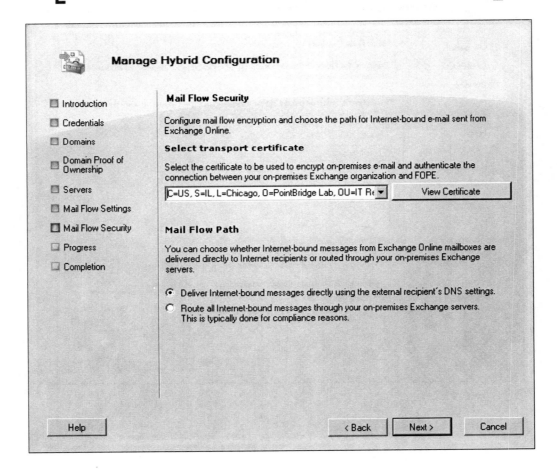

9. In the next screen that appears, click on **Manage** to set the configuration:

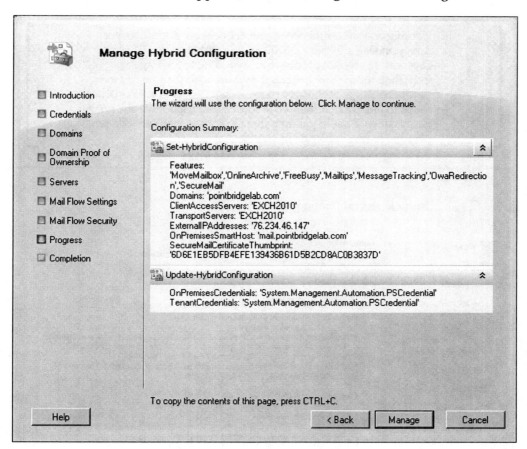

10. During the configuration:
    - ° Organization Relationships between on-premise and Office 365 are created
    - ° FOPE Inbound/Outbound Connectors are created
    - ° MRSProxy is enabled (required for mailbox moves)
    - ° E-mail alias is added to the default domain policy

11. Now click on **Finish**, to complete the installation:

If configuration errors occur, check to ensure Autodiscover is responding and your certificate is valid for Autodiscover. One way to check Autodiscover would be to leverage an Exchange testing site provided by Microsoft (`https://www.testexchangeconnectivity.com`). In addition to certificates, check to ensure that the two accounts you used have the proper permissions. Finally validate that Outlook Anywhere access is possible to this server from outside.

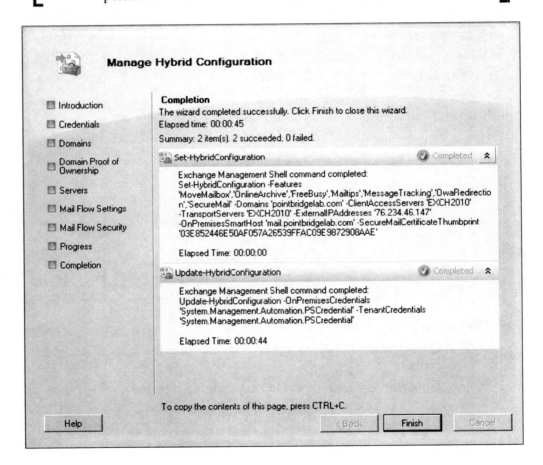

12. Now verify the organization relationship was created. In the on-premise Exchange Organization, navigate to **Organization Configuration | Organization Relationships**. You should see a **On Premise to Exchange Online** relationship, as shown in the following screenshot:

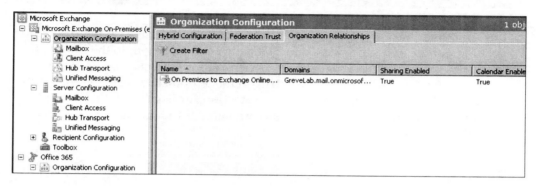

13. Now check the Office 365 organization configuration under your Office 365 subscription. Go to **Organization Configuration | Organization Relationships**. You should see a **Exchange Online to on premises...** relationship, as shown in the following screenshot:

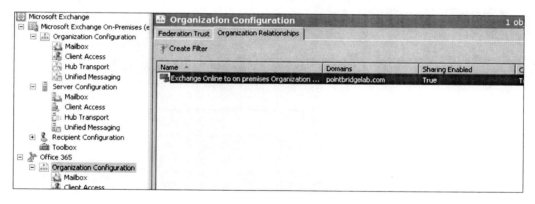

14. Verify that MRSProxy is enabled. To do this, open the Exchange Management Shell with an elevated prompt and enter the following command:

```
get-webservicesvirtualdirectory | fl Name, MRSProxyEnabled
```

The result of the preceding command is shown in the following screenshot:

```
[PS] C:\Windows\system32>get-webservicesvirtualdirectory | fl Name, MRSProxyEnabled

Name            : EWS (Default Web Site)
MRSProxyEnabled : True
```

15. Verify that the **Forefront Online Protection For Exchange (FOPE)** Inbound/Outbound Connectors were automatically created. Log in to the Portal at `https://portal.microsoftonline.com/admin` and click on **Manage Exchange Online**, find **Mail Control** on the left quick launch. On the right-hand side, select **Forefront Online Protection for Exchange**. You should now see two Hybrid connectors, inbound and outbound, as shown in the following screenshot:

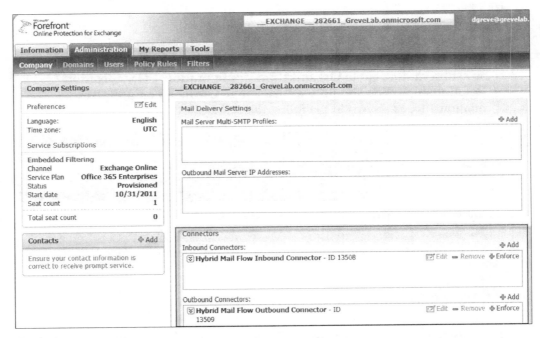

This completes our Exchange Hybrid configuration. If you were able to validate all settings, no additional steps are required for the Hybrid configuration.

Summary

In this chapter we learned how to build our third core integration point, Exchange Hybrid, to enable rich coexistence and simplify the migration to Office 365. This key integration point will allow us to leverage Office 365, as if it were an extension of our on-premise Exchange Organization.

In the next chapter, we will learn how to leverage all the integration points to start migrating mailboxes from on-premise to Office 365.

11
Performing a Hybrid Migration

Now that we have implemented all of the core integration components for Office 365, it's time to start testing and performing the migrations of mailboxes. There are many ways to perform migrations or even account provisioning. Our focus will be to perform migrations from the Exchange Management Console or by running PowerShell cmdlets. Before we get started, let's make sure your end users are ready for the migration. Once we validate the end users' readiness, we will perform both types of migrations. Specifically, we will cover the following:

- Preparing the end user for Office 365
- Performing a migration from the Exchange Management Console
- Performing a migration using PowerShell cmdlets

Preparing the end user for Office 365

There are two primary ways to deploy updates to the end users, in preparation for Office 365. Those two ways include:

- End user self-deployment
- Distribution from a software deployment service

End user self-deployment

In the end user self-deployment method, the end user navigates to the Office 365 portal and runs the Office 365 Desktop Setup:

1. To simplify the process, you would provide your users with the URL (`https://portal.microsoftonline.com/download`) that takes them directly to the **Downloads** page. The user will have to log on with their Active Directory account, as the Portal will now be using ADFS for all user accounts that were synchronized to Office 365. Please note that local admin privileges will be required to run the desktop setup.

2. Once the users enter this page, they will be able to see what is available for installation. If you have not altered the user's licenses, prior to the user navigating to this link, the user will see only the Office 365 setup wizard:

3. If you plan to deploy the Office suite from Office 365 and Lync, then you may want to license the users you are migrating for those services. By doing this the user will have more installation options as they prepare for Office 365. To assign licenses, let's log on as an admin to the portal (`https://portal.microsoftonline.com/admin`). Navigate to **Management | Users**:

4. Click on the user you wish to enable. On the **Licenses** tab, enable all the licenses you plan to assign to this user:

5. Now navigate to the **Settings** tab and set the user's location:

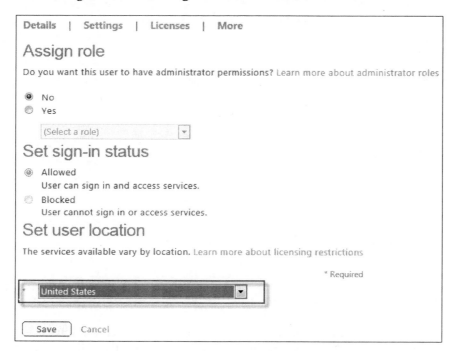

6. Once you have completed these steps, click on **Save**. You should get a warning that the user will not show up in Exchange Online, until the user is migrated. If you do not get this warning, this user may not have a mailbox on premise or you may have enabled an account that is not synchronized.

   In this example, we enabled a user with all licenses in the E3 plan. When the user navigates to this page now, he/she will see more install options:

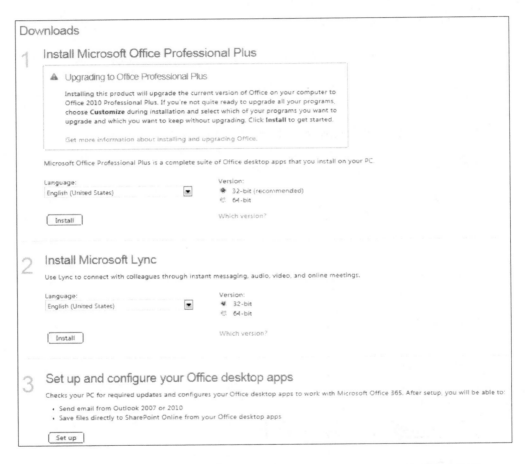

7. At this point, the user can install Office Pro Plus, Lync, and Office 365 Desktop Setup. Our focus in this example will be on the Office 365 Desktop Setup's step 3, **Set up and configure your Office desktop apps**.

   Prior to running this setup, it's highly recommended the user runs all of the latest Windows updates. In addition, the user will need local administrative access to their computer.

8. Once this is done, the user can run the Office 365 Desktop Setup found in step 3, **Set up and configure your Office desktop apps**. As you start to run through the install process, the user will be presented with configuration and install options. If you have enabled all licenses, the user will be able to configure each application within the Office 365 Desktop Setup:

9. As the mailbox has not technically been migrated to Exchange Online, you will notice **Manual steps required** listed in the installation. You can safely ignore this, if your end users are running this step before they have been migrated. This installer will also apply necessary updates for Office, Outlook, and Lync. In addition, a Sign-in Assistant will be installed for Office 365.

10. Once an administrator migrates these users' mailboxes, the end users will be notified when their Outlook client is ready to be reconfigured for the new services.

Distribution from a Software Deployment Service

Larger organizations typically do not allow local administrative access to workstations. Because of this, Microsoft has provided a list of required updates for the end user's workstation. These updates can be found here at `http://community.office365.com/en-us/w/administration/manually-install-office-365-desktop-updates.aspx`. Specifically for Exchange Online, it's important that Office/Outlook has the most recent service pack applied. Validation of the Office and Outlook updates listed in the preceding link and the deployment of Microsoft Online Sign-in Assistant. Some methods to deploy these updates can be deployed through:

- **Group Policy Object (GPO)**
- **System Center Configuration Manager (SCCM)**
- Related software management/deployment software

These updates can all be applied anytime prior to the migration of these users.

Performing a migration from the Exchange Management Console

Performing a migration from the **Exchange Management Console (EMC)** is relatively simple, as long as the Exchange Hybrid configuration has been validated and is functional:

1. To get started, connect to the Exchange Hybrid server you set up for Office 365. Open the EMC on this server. You should see both your on-premise organization and the Office 365 organization you created for the Hybrid configuration:

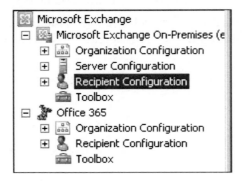

Ensure both organizations can be expanded.

2. Now navigate to the on-premise Organization and navigate to **Recipient Configuration | Mailbox**. Find a mailbox you would like to migrate. Right-click on this mailbox and click on **New Remote Move Request...**:

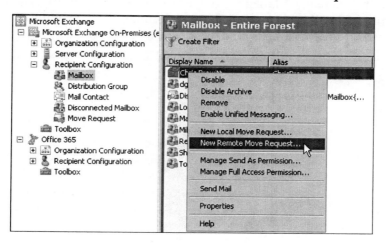

3. If the user has an Exchange archive and you plan to move this archive with the Exchange mailbox, be sure to select the **Move both the mailbox and the archive** option. Otherwise, ensure that **Move only the User mailbox** is selected and click on **Next**:

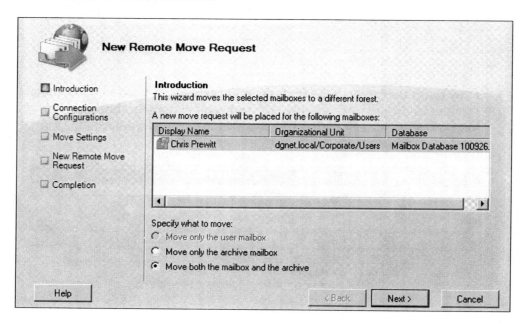

4. Ensure the **Target forest** field lists the **Office 365** forest you created for the Hybrid configuration within the EMC. Now enter the FQDN of your local Exchange 2010 hybrid server, you set up the Hybrid configuration with. In our example it is **mail.pointbridgelab.com**. Additionally, if you did not log on to the Exchange Management Console as an on-premise organization admin, you will need to enter those credentials by checking the **Use the following source forest's credential**. Click on **Next**:

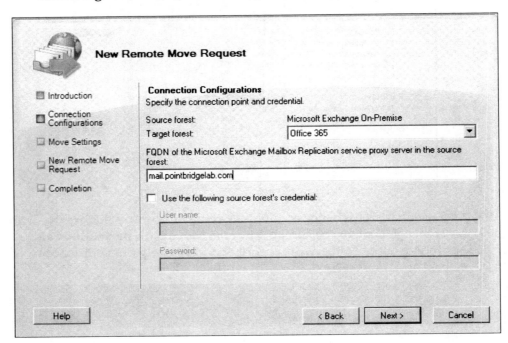

5. Now select the target delivery domain by clicking on **Browse**. This domain is not your on-premise domain, but your remote domain starting with **<subscription name>.mail.onmicrosoft.com**. It's also similar to the **Target Delivery Domain**:

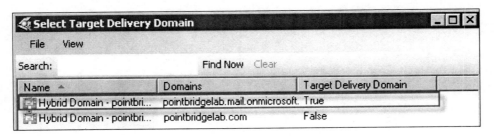

6. Once the target domain is selected, click on **Next**:

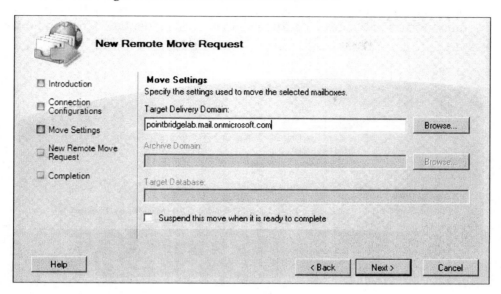

7. Validate the remote and target domains and click on **New**:

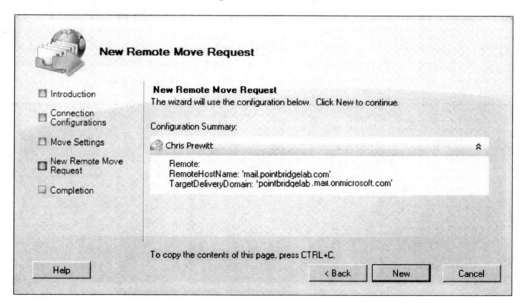

8. If you get prompted for authentication, enter your global admin or organization admin account for your Office 365 subscription. If the process fails, go back and consider adding source forest credentials. Click on **Finish**:

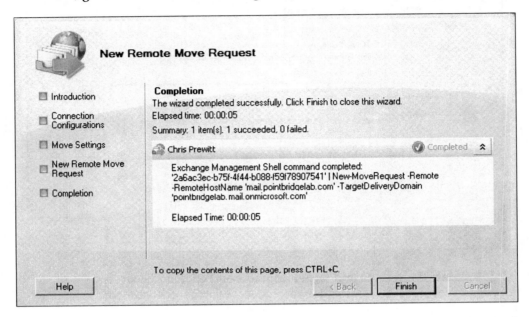

9. To view the move process, go to **Office 365** organization in EMC, expand the **Recipient Configuration**, and click on **Move Request**. In this window, you can view the migration process and see whether it is complete:

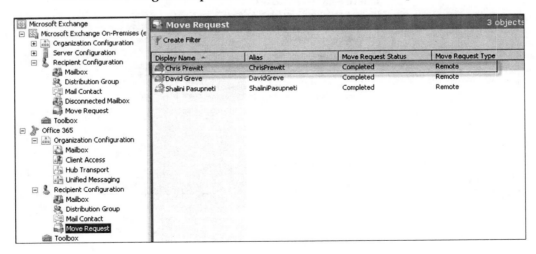

10. Once the move request is complete, you can check that the end user was migrated properly by having them logged on to Outlook or Outlook Web Access. If the user logs on to Outlook, he/she will notice they are in a disconnected state. After a short period of time, usually seconds, the user will get prompted to authenticate to his/her mailbox. It's critical they enter their UPN for logon (for ADFS) and their Active Directory password:

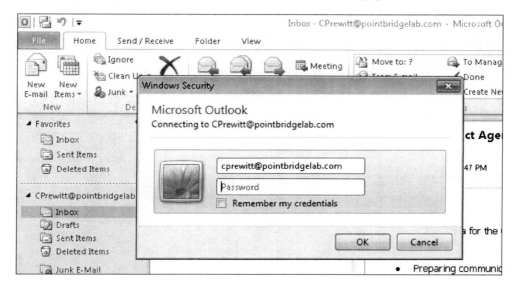

11. Once they enter their credentials and click on **OK**, they will receive a message that an administrator made a change and that Outlook will need to be restarted:

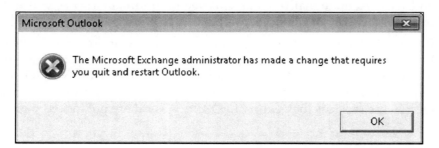

12. Once the user restarts Outlook, they should be connected to their Exchange Online mailbox. In some occasions, if the user had Outlook open during the migration, the user may have to restart Outlook more than once (they may get prompted that an administrator made a change, twice.)

13. If you would like to validate that the Outlook client is connected to the Exchange Online mailbox, you can do so by looking at the account server settings. An example of these settings is as follows:

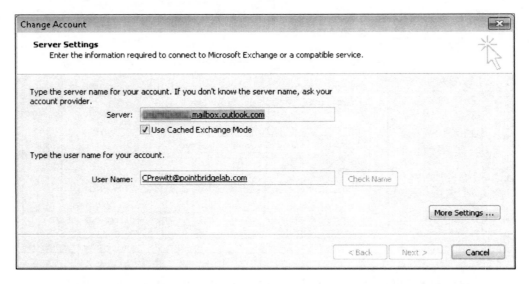

14. You can repeat this process and perform bulk migrations by selecting multiple users. To do so, just select multiple users before you right-click and select **Remote mailbox move**. When migrating in a scale, you should consider an array of Client Access Servers to boost migration speeds.

15. Finally, if you have not already done so, apply the appropriate Exchange licenses to the mailboxes you migrated. The mailboxes will function in Office 365 for a short period of time, without those licenses. However, it is very important that you apply the appropriate licenses right away, so the users receive the services they expect in Office 365 and are not locked out.

Performing a migration using PowerShell cmdlets

The move process from the Exchange Management Console (EMC) is technically all PowerShell driven, on the backend. The EMC allows administrators to simplify the process of performing quick migrations to Office 365. As all of these commands are PowerShell driven, let's review how to perform a migration without the EMC. We will cover the following areas:

- Assigning a license to a user with PowerShell
- Migrating a user to Office 365 with PowerShell
- Migrating users in bulk to Office 365 with PowerShell

Assigning a license to a user with PowerShell

Let's first look at applying licenses through PowerShell:

1. To do so, start by installing the Online Services Module found at `http://onlinehelp.microsoft.com/en-us/Office365-enterprises/ff652560.aspx`

2. Go to step 2, **Download the Microsoft Online Services Module**, and either install the 32-bit or 64-bit version:

2. Download the Microsoft Online Services Module

The Microsoft Online Services Module for Windows PowerShell is a download that comes with Office 365. This module installs a set of cmdlets to Windows PowerShell; you run those cmdlets to set up single sign-on for Office 365. Before you set up single sign-on in your full production environment, you can also run a single sign-on pilot. See Run a pilot to test single sign-on before setting it up (optional).

- Download the 32-bit module
- Download the 64-bit module

Note:

- For more information about a cmdlet that you can run in Windows PowerShell, at the Windows PowerShell command prompt, type `Get-help` and the name of the cmdlet.
- For more information about single sign-on cmdlets, see Use Windows PowerShell to manage Office 365.

3. Now connect to your Office 365 subscription by running the following cmdlets:

   ° `$cred=get-credential`

   Enter your Office365 administrator credentials when prompted.

   ° `Connect-msolservice –credential $cred`

4. Let's capture the licenses that are assigned to your tenant by running the cmdlet to gather those licenses:

   ```
   Get-msolsubscription | select skupartnumber, totallicenses | ft -
   autosize
   ```

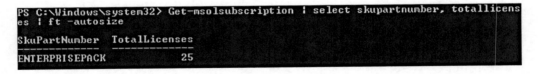

5. In our example, the ENTERPRISEPACK licenses are available, which is an E3 license. Now let's assign a license to a user. To do so, we need to first assign the country location. The following syntax shows how to do this:

   ```
   set-msoluser –userprincipalname "UPN of User" –usagelocation
   "Country Code"
   ```

For example, see the following command:

```
set-msoluser -userprincipalname "dgreve@pointbridgelab.com" -
usagelocation US
```

6. Now we can assign the license by using the following syntax:

```
set-msoluserlicense -userprincipalname "UPN of User" -addlicenses
"TenantName:License Name"
```

For example, see the following command:

```
set-msoluserlicense -userprincipalnamedgreve@pointbridgelab.com -
addlicensesPointBridgeLab:ENTERPRISEPACK
```

7. To verify that the license was applied properly, run the following command:

```
get-msoluser -userprincipalname "UPN of User" | select
Licenses,IsLicensed | fl
```

The returned results should show the license you assigned to the user:

```
PS C:\> get-msoluser -userprincipalname dgreve@pointbridgelab.com : select Licen
ses,IsLicensed : fl


Licenses    : {GreveLab:ENTERPRISEPACK}
IsLicensed : True
```

Now you can apply licenses to users in bulk by using a CSV method for importing user names to PowerShell cmdlets.

Migrating a user to Office 365 with PowerShell

Let's now perform a migration from on-premise to Office 365. To do so, follow these steps:

1. Let's connect to a PowerShell session on a computer you have administrative access to.

> If you run this from the Exchange Hybrid server, be sure to unload the Exchange snap-in for PowerShell. If you do not, these cmdlets will not function properly.

Ensure that you are running the PowerShell session as an administrator.

2. Now, let's connect to the Office 365 subscription. Enter the following commands in the command prompt:

   ° `set-executionpolicy unrestricted`
   ° `$LiveCred = Get-Credential`

Enter your Office 365 global admin credentials

- ○ `$Session = New-PSSession -ConfigurationNameMicrosoft. Exchange -ConnectionUri https://ps.outlook.com/ powershell/ -Credential $LiveCred -Authentication Basic -AllowRedirection`
- ○ `Import-PSSession $Session`
- ○ `$RemoteCredential= Get-Credential`

 Provide your on-premise organization admin credentials.

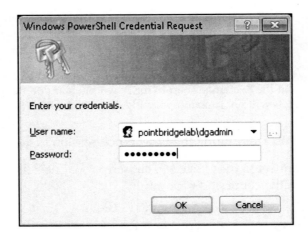

3. Now let's start the actual migration of a mailbox:

```
New-MoveRequest -Identity (UPN of User) -Remote -RemoteHostName
(your on-premise Exchange Hybrid Server) -TargetDeliveryDomain
(Hybrid Subscription Domain) -RemoteCredential $RemoteCredential
```

4. To verify the progress of a mailbox, you can run the `get-moverequest`
   `cmdlet` to determine if the migration is complete:

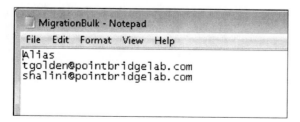

If you did not assign a country code or license to this user, prior to migration, you should now apply the appropriate licenses to the users you migrated.

Migrating users in bulk to Office 365 with PowerShell

Now that we learned how to migrate users with PowerShell, let's perform these same steps, but now migrating users with a CSV file for bulk migrations. As always, when migrating in scale, you should consider an array of Client Access Servers, to boost migration speeds:

1. To get started, let's first create our CSV file. To do so, create a file with a header, **Alias** and add the identity for each user you choose to migrate in each row:

2. Now, create a PS1 file in Notepad and insert the following lines in it. The highlighted part will differ as per your settings:

```
$mbxlist = Import-CSV c:\csv\migrationbulk.csv
foreach ($line in $mbxlist) {
New-MoveRequest -Identity $line.alias -Remote -RemoteHostName
mail.pointbridgelab.com -TargetDeliveryDomain pointbridgelab.mail.
onmicrosoft.com -RemoteCredential $RemoteCredential
}
```

3. Now follow all the steps in the previous section, up to `new-moverequest`. Instead of running `new-moverequest`, call the PS1 file you created with the preceding step. Once you call this file, you will see each mailbox move process start until the last alias in your CSV file is complete.

   Additionally, you can also add all the previous commands to connect to the service, right to this PS1 file, making it easier to quickly execute bulk migrations to Office 365.

Summary

Throughout this chapter we reviewed the various ways to license and migrate users in an Exchange Hybrid configuration, from on-premise Exchange to Exchange Online. We learned about migrations from on-premise while leveraging the Exchange Management Console, as well as through PowerShell cmdlets.

In the next chapter, we will learn about cleanup activities we can perform, after we complete al! migrations to Office 365 from Exchange on premise.

12
Post Migration Considerations

By now we have a good understanding of how to prepare for, deploy, and start the process of migrating mailboxes. Before we get too far down the path of migrations, let's consider some additional changes that may be required to either support a complete move to Office 365 or a long-term coexistence strategy.

As we approach finalizing our migrations to Office 365, let's review some on-premise changes that may be necessary. These may include:

- On-premise resources changes
    ° Shared mailboxes
    ° Conference rooms
    ° Public folders

- Changing your MX record in a Hybrid configuration

On-premise resource changes

With most Exchange Organizations, we may be leveraging various types of resource mailboxes or Public folders. When you start migrating users to Office 365, your Office 365 users will lose access to these delegated resources. If the resource is a conference room, the user will still be able to book time on that conference room and view the existing schedules; however, that's the extent of management for those resource objects. Public folders are completely inaccessible from an Office 365 mailbox.

While you migrate on-premise mailboxes, you may need to consider moving these resources with the users moving to Office 365. Let's cover these various resources and how you need to prepare for their moves to Office 365. The resources we will cover are:

- Shared mailboxes
- Conference rooms
- Public folders

Shared mailboxes

If you are leveraging on-premise shared mailboxes today, then you may want, or need, to migrate them to Office 365. Typically, if the shared mailbox is accessed by other users, and not an application, you should consider moving the shared mailboxes with those users accessing them. Before you move the mailbox, it's important that we confirm that the shared mailbox is actually listed as a shared mailbox and not a standard user mailbox. To set an on-premise mailbox to a shared mailbox, simply run the following PowerShell cmdlet from an Exchange 2010 Management Shell:

```
Set-mailbox Alias -type:shared
```

Once you have confirmed that the mailbox is set to shared, perform a standard mailbox move to Office 365, as you would do for any other user mailbox. The reason why this step is important is that the shared mailbox will not require a license. If you move a shared mailbox to Office 365, as a user mailbox, it will require a license to be used. After you move the mailbox to Office 365, consider setting a quota on the mailbox. An example quota would be as follows:

```
Set-Mailbox Alias -ProhibitSendReceiveQuota 5GB -ProhibitSendQuota 4.75GB
-IssueWarningQuota 4.5GB
```

In order to set this quota, you need to load the Microsoft Online Services Module for PowerShell.

Alternatively you can create shared mailboxes directly in Office 365. You may want to do this after you have completely moved off of Office 365 or to simplify from creating mailboxes on-premise. You have to create a shared mailbox for the Microsoft Online Services Module for PowerShell. To do so, enter the following cmdlet:

```
New-Mailbox -Name "Display Name" -Alias Alias -Shared
```

Now that you have created the shared mailbox, think about applying a quota to it:

```
Set-Mailbox Alias -ProhibitSendReceiveQuota 5GB -ProhibitSendQuota 4.75GB
-IssueWarningQuota 4.5GB
```

After creating the shared mailbox, you can now manage and assign users from PowerShell or the Exchange Management Console.

Conference rooms

Conference rooms are very much like Shared Mailboxes. It's important that we ensure the conference room is listed as a room object prior to migrating the mailbox. If you do not list the conference room as a room object, you will require a license on the Conference Room Mailbox. To set the Conference Room as a room object, simply run the following PowerShell cmdlet from an Exchange 2010 Management Shell:

```
Set-mailbox Alias -type:room
```

Once you have confirmed that the mailbox is set to room, perform a standard mailbox move to Office 365, as you would do for any other user mailbox.

Alternatively, you can create a conference room directly in Office 365. You can do so through either PowerShell or the **Exchange Control Panel (ECP)**. The following steps demonstrate how to create a room object directly in the ECP:

1. Go to **Users & Groups**, click on **New Room Mailbox**, under **Mailboxes**:

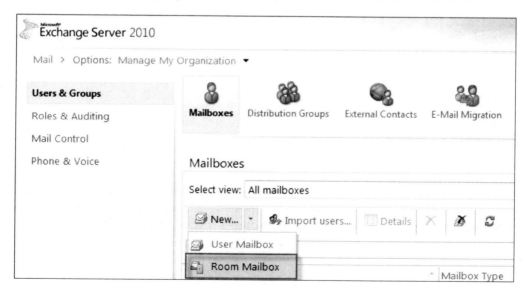

2. Enter all the details for this room. If you plan to receive e-mails on a specific domain for this room, be sure to select the correct domain alias:

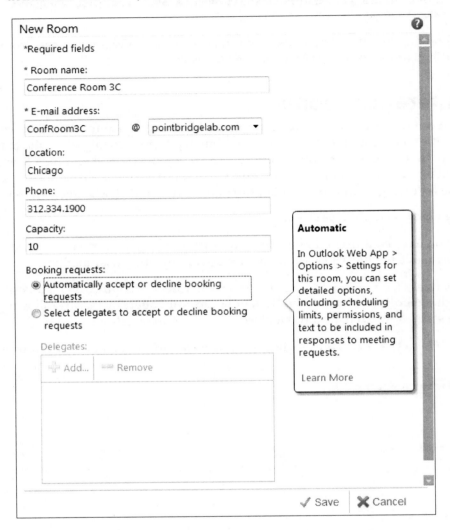

At this point, you have a bit of flexibility in how you want to configure the room. From the number of attendees in the room, to who can book it and how meetings get approved. Be sure to set the appropriate settings for your organization.

Public folders

Public folders are not supported in Office 365. In addition, any mailboxes or resources moved to Office 365 will no longer have access to public folders in a Hybrid environment. It's important that you evaluate how public folders are used and how to convert them, as referenced in *Chapter 7, Preparing for a Hybrid Deployment and Migration*. If you decide to migrate public folders to shared mailboxes, be sure to create those mailboxes as either on-premise shared mailboxes or in Office 365. If you create them on-premise, then you can use Outlook 2007 or 2010 to drag the contents from the public folder to a shared mailbox.

Changing your MX record in a Hybrid configuration

At some point you will want to consider moving your inbound mail routing from your on-premise mail system to Office 365's **ForeFront Online Protection for Exchange (FOPE)** If you do not have any on-premise gateway mail routing requirements, you may want to consider this move when most of your mailboxes are in Office 365. If you plan to do a flash cutover, then you may want to consider the MX change right away.

Moving your MX record does not mean on-premise mailboxes will stop receiving e-mails, this is why the Hybrid option is available for Exchange on-premise organizations. You may have other on-premise mail routing requirements, which should be evaluated before changing your MX record.

To get started, you first need to set up your Office 365 FOPE settings to receive e-mails. Go to the Office 365 Admin Portal at `https://portal.microsoftonline.com`. Click on **Manage** under **Exchange Online**:

Admin shortcuts

- Reset user passwords
- Add new users
- Assign user licenses
- Create a service request

Microsoft Office 365

Exchange Online
Outlook settings and protection.
Manage

Lync Online
Instant messaging with audio and video and online meetings.
Manage

1. Now, go to **Mail Control** and click on **Configure IP safelisting, perimeter message tracing, and e-mail policies.**:

2. To start, we need to review how the Hybrid inbound connector was created. Locate the Hybrid connector under **Inbound Connectors** and expand it. If the **Sender Domains** is set to ***.***, we may have to disassociate it from the service and create a new one. In the following screenshot, our domain shows ***.***:

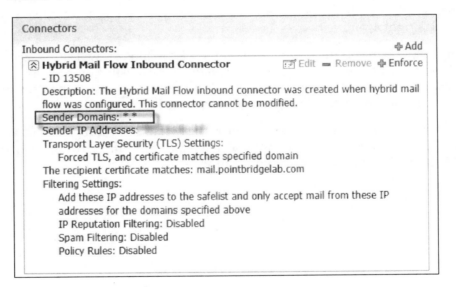

3. To disassociate the inbound connector, click on **+ Enforce**, then click on **- Release**, to disassociate it from all the domains in your tenant.

4. Now, let's create a new **Hybrid Mail Flow Inbound Connector**. To do so, click on **+ Add** besides **Inbound Connectors**:

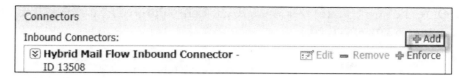

5. Now, create the new connector with the name of your choice. Copy the configuration of the existing Hybrid Mail Flow Inbound Connector, except, instead of adding **Sender Domains: *.***, change **Sender Domains** to all the Domains you host in your on-premise Exchange organization. You may create your new connector, as shown in the following screenshot:

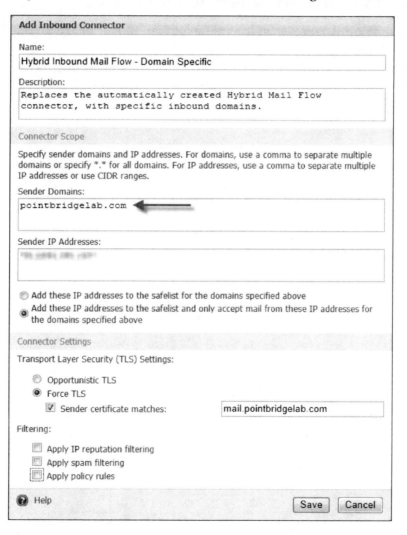

6. Once the new connector is created, click on **+ Enforce** to associate it to the domains you specified:

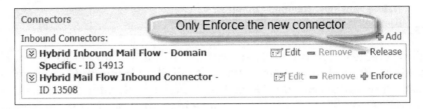

Inbound Hybrid mail flow should be functional again.

7. We now need to create an Internet mail flow connector. To do so, click on **+ Add** besides **Inbound Connectors**.

8. On the new connector, let's configure it for all inbound mail. The following example demonstrates the configuration of a general inbound internet mail:

9. Once the new connector is created, click on **+ Enforce** to associate it to all domains.

10. Now, the only connectors that should be enforced are the two new connectors we created. To validate if your domain(s) have the inbound connectors associated to them, go to **Administration | Domains**:

11. Now select your primary e-mail domain. You should only see the two new connectors associated to it under **Inbound Connectors**:

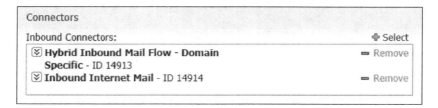

At this point, I would consider waiting up to 24 hours, before changing your MX record. This way you allow FOPE to replicate to all FOPE datacenters. Ensure that you perform testing to validate that the inbound/outbound Hybrid mail continues to work.

Once you are ready to change your MX record, the process is somewhat simple. Go to the Office 365 Admin Portal at `https://portal.microsoftonline.com` and follow these steps:

1. Click on **Domains** in the left navigation:

2. Now select the domain you want to change your MX record for and click on **View DNS Settings**:

3. On the new page, you should see what your MX record should be changed to. Update your external DNS settings to this new MX record:

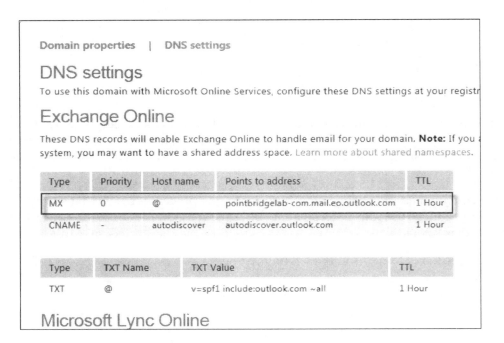

After you update your MX record wait for DNS to replicate, and then start testing the mail flow from Internet e-mail accounts to your Office 365 and on-premise mailboxes. If you set up the connectors properly and DNS has had a chance to replicate, all mail should be going through Office 365 and either delivered to an Office 365 mailbox or traversed over the Hybrid connectors and to your on-premise mailboxes.

Summary

Resources play an important role in any migration or move to Office 365. This role includes how users leverage these resources. We learned how to migrate these resources to Office 365, allowing users to continue to leverage these resources and minimizing the downtime while the users are in transition.

In the next chapter, we will provide references to materials that support and provide additional information on your move to Office 365.

References

Whether we are a Small Business or an Enterprise, we learned how to perform migrations by leveraging various scenarios our business state may be in. From simple to rich integration with Exchange Online, Office 365 offers many opportunities for our organizations to quickly integrate and deploy services. As our business grows, the services enables us the flexibility to take advantage of small or large rapid growth, offering federation with other businesses, rapid licensing of a small or large number of mailboxes to quick acquisition provisioning. We can apply the information that we gained from what we have learned to management and future growth of the new service.

Much of what we learned was from a combination of experience, existing documentation, and knowledge sharing. In the following sections, you will find references to further reading or the supporting documentations.

Office 365

- **Service descriptions** (for all Office 365 services): `http://www.microsoft.com/download/en/details.aspx?id=13602`

- **Office 365 support**: `http://community.office365.com/en-us/default.aspx`

- **Microsoft Online team blog**: `http://community.office365.com/en-us/b/office_365_technical_blog/default.aspx`

- **Microsoft Office 365 Readiness Tool**: `http://community.office365.com/f/183/p/2285/8155.aspx#8155`

- **Office 365 Integration Module for Windows Small Business Server 2011 Essentials**: `http://www.microsoft.com/download/en/details.aspx?id=28566`

- **Setting up a shared mailbox**: `http://technet.microsoft.com/en-us/exchangelabshelp/ee441202`

Exchange

- **Microsoft Exchange Server 2010**: http://technet.microsoft.com/en-us/library/bb124558.aspx

- **Microsoft Exchange Server team blog**: http://msexchangeteam.com

- **Prepare Active Directory and domains**: http://technet.microsoft.com/en-us/library/bb125224.aspx

- **Office 365 synchronized attributes**: http://support.microsoft.com/default.aspx?scid=kb;en-US;2256198

- **Exchange Server Active Directory Schema Changes Reference, November 2011**: http://www.microsoft.com/downloads/en/details.aspx?FamilyID=3d44de93-3f21-44d0-a0a1-35ff5dbabd0b&displaylang=en

- **Using Windows PowerShell to manage Office 365**: http://onlinehelp.microsoft.com/office365-enterprises/hh124998.aspx

Third-party tools or add-ons

- **Quest Migration Manager for Exchange** (when you cannot perform a Hybrid integration): http://www.quest.com/migration-manager-for-exchange/

- **MigrationWiz** (migrating from multiple messaging systems): http://www.migrationwiz.com

- **Exchange Hosted Encryption**: http://www.microsoft.com/online/exchange-email-encryption.aspx

- **Right Management Server**: http://technet.microsoft.com/en-us/library/cc179103.aspx

- **Exchange Online Archive**: http://technet.microsoft.com/en-us/library/hh529934.aspx

- **Proofpoint Data Loss Prevention (DLP)**: http://www.proofpoint.com/products/privacy/index.php

- **Migrating from Lotus Notes**
  - **Quest**: http://www.quest.com/notes-migrator-for-exchange/
  - **Binary Tree**: http://www.binarytree.com/Solutions/Lotus-Customers/Migrate-to-Microsoft-Online/Weekend-Express.aspx

- **Migrating from GroupWise**: http://www.quest.com/groupwise-migrator-for-exchange

Authors' blogs

- **David Greve**: http://blogs.perficient.com/microsoft/author/dgreve/

- **Loryan Strant**: http://thecloudmouth.com/

Index

roles & auditing section, Exchange Online
administration interface 38

S

samAccountName attribute 58
SBS2011E
  about 43
  Office 365, connecting to 44-47
SBS2011E Dashboard
  used, for managing user accounts 49-53
security groups area, management section
  28
Select applications to configure section 138,
  160
service account
  ADFS-Admin 117
  ADFS-Auth 117
  ADFS-Service 117
service descriptions
  URL 235
service health page, support section 36
Service-level Agreements. *See* SLA
service requests page, support section 35
Set-Mailbox Alias -ProhibitSendReceive-
  Quota 5GB -ProhibitSendQuota
  4.75GB -IssueWarningQuota 4.5GB
  224
Set-Mailbox Alias -ProhibitSendReceive-
  Quota 5GB -ProhibitSendQuota
  4.75GB -IssueWarningQuota 4.5GB,
  shared , mailboxes 225
Set-Mailbox Alias -ProhibitSendReceive-
  Quota 5GB -ProhibitSendQuota
  4.75GB -IssueWarningQuota 4.5GB,
  shared mailboxes 224
Set-mailbox Alias -type:room, conference
  rooms 225
set-mailbox Alias -type:shared, shared
  mailboxes 224
setup section, Administration Overview
  interface
  about 26
  custom plan section 27
  overview page 26
shared mailbox

URL 235
shared mailboxes, on-premise resource
  changes
  about 224
  New-Mailbox -Name 225
  Set-Mailbox Alias -ProhibitSendReceive-
  Quota 5GB -ProhibitSendQuota
  4.75GB -IssueWarningQuota 4.5GB
  225
Sign-in Assistant 114
sign-up, Office 365
  process 15-19
simple migration
  about 85
  environment, preparing for 89-93
  options 86
  people considerations 89
  planning for 88
  process, in nutshell 88
  technical considerations 88, 89
simple migration, options
  comparing 87, 88
  Exchange Server 2003 or 2007 87
  Hosted Exchange or Gmail 86
  IMAP 86
  POP e-mail 86
single ADFS farm
  versus multiple farms 63
Site Bindings page 147
SLA 66
Software Deployment Service
  distribution from 210
SQl cluster server, ADFS 69
SSL certificate drop-down menu 147
staged migration
  about 87
  versus cutover migration, requisites 93
standard X.509 certificate 118
Start the ADFS Management snap-in when
  this wizard closes checkbox 136
subscription
  preparing 107-112
subscriptions section, Administration
  Overview interface
  licenses section 32
  manage page 30, 32

Thank you for buying
Microsoft Office 365: Exchange Online Implementation and Migration

About Packt Publishing

Packt, pronounced 'packed', published its first book "Mastering phpMyAdmin for Effective MySQL Management" in April 2004 and subsequently continued to specialize in publishing highly focused books on specific technologies and solutions.

Our books and publications share the experiences of your fellow IT professionals in adapting and customizing today's systems, applications, and frameworks. Our solution based books give you the knowledge and power to customize the software and technologies you're using to get the job done. Packt books are more specific and less general than the IT books you have seen in the past. Our unique business model allows us to bring you more focused information, giving you more of what you need to know, and less of what you don't.

Packt is a modern, yet unique publishing company, which focuses on producing quality, cutting-edge books for communities of developers, administrators, and newbies alike. For more information, please visit our website: www.packtpub.com.

About Packt Enterprise

In 2010, Packt launched two new brands, Packt Enterprise and Packt Open Source, in order to continue its focus on specialization. This book is part of the Packt Enterprise brand, home to books published on enterprise software – software created by major vendors, including (but not limited to) IBM, Microsoft and Oracle, often for use in other corporations. Its titles will offer information relevant to a range of users of this software, including administrators, developers, architects, and end users.

Writing for Packt

We welcome all inquiries from people who are interested in authoring. Book proposals should be sent to author@packtpub.com. If your book idea is still at an early stage and you would like to discuss it first before writing a formal book proposal, contact us; one of our commissioning editors will get in touch with you.

We're not just looking for published authors; if you have strong technical skills but no writing experience, our experienced editors can help you develop a writing career, or simply get some additional reward for your expertise.

Microsoft Exchange 2010
PowerShell Cookbook

Manage and maintain your Microsoft Exchange 2010
environment with Windows PowerShell 2.0 and the
Exchange Management Shell

Mike Pfeiffer

Microsoft Exchange 2010 PowerShell Cookbook

ISBN: 978-1-84968-246-6   Paperback: 480 pages

Manage and maintain your Microsoft Exchange 2010
environment with Windows PowerShell 2.0 and the
Exchange Management Shell

1. Step-by-step instructions on how to write
    scripts for nearly every aspect of Exchange 2010
    including the Client Access Server, Mailbox,
    and Transport server roles

2. Understand the core concepts of Windows
    PowerShell 2.0 that will allow you to write
    sophisticated scripts and one-liners used with
    the Exchange Management Shell

3. Learn how to write scripts and functions,
    schedule scripts to run automatically, and
    generate complex reports

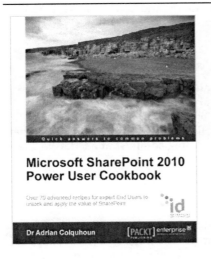

Microsoft SharePoint 2010
Power User Cookbook

Over 70 advanced recipes for expert End Users to
unlock and apply the value of SharePoint

Dr Adrian Colquhoun

Microsoft SharePoint 2010 Power User Cookbook

ISBN: 978-1-84968-288-6   Paperback: 344 pages

Over 70 advanced recipes for expert End Users to
unlock and apply the real value of SharePoint

1. Discover how to apply SharePoint far beyond
    basic functionality

2. Explore the Business Intelligence capabilities of
    SharePoint with KPIs and custom dashboards

3. Take a deep dive into document management,
    data integration, electronic forms, and
    workflow scenarios

Please check **www.PacktPub.com** for information on our titles

Microsoft SharePoint 2010 and
Windows PowerShell 2.0: Expert
Cookbook

ISBN: 978-1-84968-410-1   Paperback: 310 pages

50 advanced recipes for administrators and IT Pros
to master Microsoft SharePoint 2010 and Microsoft
PowerShell 2.0 automation

1. Dive straight into expert recipes for SharePoint
    and PowerShell administration without dwelling
    on the basics

2. Master how to administer BCS in SharePoint,
    automate the configuration of records
    management features, create custom PowerShell
    cmdlets, and much more in this book and e-book

3. A hands-on cookbook focusing on only the
    most high level tips and tricks for mastering
    SharePoint and PowerShell administration

iPhone with Microsoft Exchange
Server 2010: Business Integration
and Deployment

ISBN: 978-1-84969-148-2   Paperback: 290 pages

Set up Microsoft Exchange Server 2010 and deploy
iPhones and other iDevices securely into your
business

1. Learn about Apple's mobile devices and how
    they work with Exchange Server 2010

2. Plan and deploy a highly available Exchange
    organization and Office 365 tenant

3. Create and enforce security policies and set up
    certificate-based authentication

Please check **www.PacktPub.com** for information on our titles

Lightning Source UK Ltd.
Milton Keynes UK
UKOW021120260313

208197UK00004B/137/P